A Wicke

C000246221

A Wicked Fist

A true story of prison and freedom

Eve McDougall

Wild Goose Publications

This book is dedicated to Lady Martha Bruce and all who, like her, are devoted to prison reform in the belief that 'the loss of freedom is punishment enough'.

Also to Gary Noble and my four children whose beliefs and faith in me helped write this book, and to all the people who have supported me at different times in my life to date.

And a special thank you to Martha Bruce and John Harvey for their written contribution to the book.

The great thing about the word love,
It never ends.

inspired by Martha Bruce and John Harvey

Justice hit me with a wicked fist
locked me in a prison
put me on a list

From *Back to My Homeland* by E. McD.

Contents

Introduction
Lady Martha Bruce

I am honoured to have been invited to contribute to this book. It is the true story of a girl who, by her own determination and growing self-insight, despite enormous difficulties and setbacks, has developed into a mature adult now able to advise, help and support others less able than herself.

Eve's story raises many issues of interest not only to those working in the fields of penal affairs, after-care, rehabilitation and delinquency, but also to people who have come up against difficulties in their experiences of custody and their fight against dependencies. She is a living example of someone who has turned her own corner, understanding and learning to trust the power of God's forgiveness.

Our paths crossed initially when I was Governor of Gateside Prison, Greenock, then Scotland's only prison for women and additionally housing a Borstal institution, a Young Offenders institution and a small male remand wing.

I joined the Scottish Prison Service in 1968, by the back door as it were. In those days the women's service was a separate entity and direct entry to an Assistant Governor grade was via a Civil Service interview.

My previous working life had been in the Army and Territorial Army and my interests had always been centred in people: assessing potential, building teams and trying to help others achieve. The Prison Service advertisement coincided with the demise of my part of the Territorial Army. I applied and was successful in obtaining the post at Greenock as an Assistant Governor on probation. After two years I was appointed Governor in charge.

I first met Eve when she had been sentenced to two years' residential training under Section 58A of the Children and Young Persons (Scotland) Act and, because of her history as an absconder and the fact that no secure accommodation for girls existed, she had been sent to us. Prison under this section of the Act was deemed a place of safety, but with what consequences?

During the period of the late '60s/early '70s we were called on to look after over twelve of these young girls, but only Eve has kept in regular touch with me. Her story tells of some of our subsequent meetings and correspondence.

I have a strong belief that relationships and friendship form the basis of trust and growing awareness. Eve, as others in her predicament, found it exceedingly difficult to trust. My part in her story is only a small one. She has worked at her own life and, with growing insight, has been able to use other agencies in what she explains as her 'up-rising'. Such agencies do exist. It is just a pity that the criminal justice system, after-care, caring and dependency organisations are not better co-ordinated and geared to help prevent offending.

At the end of this book I will elaborate on some of the issues Eve's account raises and give an update on any progress there has been in the system in the last twenty years.

These have been twenty years in which Eve has experienced the depths of despair but, with God's help and her own determination and the support of those who love her, she has come through and been able to tell us her story.

A Wicked Fist

The earth that I walk on
is my pride and joy,
I love it to bits,
just like a toy.

The Break In

Once upon a time in a small town in Scotland a child was born. The date: April 1, 1957. Yes, All Fools' day, that's me.

This is how the story goes. It was winter here. I'm sure you have heard about the Scottish weather – it's punishment. I had just been released from an approved school, after spending my fourteenth year incarcerated. Now fifteen, fleeing drunk, starving with hunger, I saw this baker's shop and staggered over. I looked in. There were cakes, pies and buns inside. I booted the door straight in, stepped through the big hole and walked over to the food. To my horror they were ornaments! Every piece in the window was a dummy.

What a joke! I should have remembered All Fools' day . . .

Police Cell

Oh, no! It was the police panda car pulling up outside the baker's shop. I jumped in a cupboard, trying to hide. The police pulled me out and they put me in the panda car.

A doomed, sick feeling came over me. I tried to sober up from my drunken stupor. By now the police were laughing at me staggering about trying to keep my balance. I started shouting at the police with abusive language. About four of them grabbed me by the arms and threw me into a panda car, at the same time pushing me. I couldn't really feel it. The police got me to Mill Street police station, they punched and kicked me, then chucked me into a cell. When I awoke from my drunken sleep, my head was pounding and my body . . . oh, it felt like it had been dragged through a hedge.

Then I remembered what I had done . . . ! My God, thought I, this is not good, I'm in big trouble. I was sitting in the corner recalling last night when the police had chucked me in the cell and one of them said, 'We will make sure you get locked up this time, McDougall.' I felt those words cut like a sword. The nightmare had begun; from deep down in my soul I had a terrible doomed feeling that the police were right. I was going to be locked away in an over-twenty-ones' prison, my only crime being that I was fifteen and hungry.

The police went to inform my mum that I would be staying in the police station till Monday morning. I was let out of the cell to wash myself; later they gave me tea and cold toast. As I bit into the bread, I wondered if the dummy cakes would have tasted better, then I threw up over the floor. A big polisman unlocked the cell door, telling me my mum was here for a visit. He looked at the mess on the floor and said, 'You'll need a bucket and mop.'

Mum told me that the police had said, 'Eve is unruly like an animal running wild,' and yes, they could keep me in the cells for a weekend. My poor mum was powerless and unable to do a thing to get me out of that horrible police station.

All I could say to her was, 'I'm so sorry to put you through this stress.' Mum cried out, 'You shouldn't be locked up for such a foolish crime, you're only fifteen.' It was my social worker, Miss Cool, who kept saying I was unruly – she wanted me locked away. It was her who had me put into an approved school for over a year. Miss Cool and I never got on from the second we met. I tried, but if I had known what was to come, I would never have bothered. Cool hated the sight of me, her eyes told me that. Every time she fired those cold daggers at me, I really wanted to spit on her face.

Police cell
The light bulb stays on all the time,
The brain damage is a crime,
The life in here is not worth a dime,
Let me out or give me time.

On the way to the Paisley Sheriff Court, I was thinking Cool + McDougall = loss of freedom. It was never McDougall against sheriff, it was always Cool against McDougall, and the doomed feeling inside my heart told me 'goodbye home, sweet home'. The nightmare was getting closer as the police van turned into the back of the court hoose.

The Sheriff Court

God, this was it! I'm going to be locked away. These words would not leave me, they were haunting me. Waiting in the court cell it was freezing cold. I smoked like a lum. When my lawyer informed me that the social worker had put in the worst report about me, it didn't surprise me at all.

I knew she had never liked me anyway. My last memory of her that day was of her talking and laughing with the police. Yes, she had just put the icing on the dummy cakes, and I was the fool right enough.

I waited for a short while, my heart pounding scared, not knowing what was really to come. My name was called, and I was led into the courtroom and told to sit in the dock. The charge was read out. My lawyer got up and spoke about me being just fifteen years old, but nobody listened to him. The judge said, 'Stand, McDougall. You are remanded for three weeks in Gateside prison; you will go to H.M.P. Gateside, Greenock.' I found out later it's called a C.Y.P. Act 1968, meaning children, young persons. I was in total confusion. I looked round at my mum, and she shouted out: 'You can't do this, it's not right.' Mother's shouts did no good. They could do this, and they did. I felt nothing after that. I was right, I was doomed.

Remanded to Prison

It was December 2, 1972, and bitter cold. Oh God . . . ! What is to become of me? I'm going to be locked up with Scotland's most notorious convicts. I didn't want to think about it any more. It was really scary; I had to be brave. There were so many terrible stories about this jail, the only women's prison in Scotland.

People had been hung in this prison, men and women; the place was nearly a hundred years old. One of its nicknames is Colditz; the reason being that it stands on a hill, with the biting Scottish winds blowing all around it.

The police loaded us up into the van and it was off to the prison. One of the coppers said to me: 'I told you, McDougall, you were going to jail.' I felt tearful. I wanted my mum. I looked up through the dark greyness of the sky, and my heavy heart said goodbye to Paisley. The journey to the prison took over an hour. I sat there remembering the look on my mum's face, and I so much wanted to burst out greetin.

I didn't cry in front of the polis. I just could not show these people any kind of emotion; and above all, I was a McDougall . . . !

Aye, it was a bloody tragedy. How can these people lock me away in a jail? I had a terrible hangover, my body was in severe pain all over, and my sad heart felt so let down by these adults. If this is an example my elders are showing me, I'd rather die young than grow up like that.

I was confused as we drove to Gateside. It didn't feel real, it had to be an illusion. The Children and Young Persons Act felt like some sick law that incarcerates children. I wasn't looking forward to Gateside. My past life started to flash in front of me.

My Young Life

My first vision of being in the world . . . It was at my Aunt Greta's hoose, near the Barrhead train station. Her daughter Annie was very close to us in those days. I remember being in my pram; Mum was sorting the reins on to me. I must have been about ten months old. I was slavering at the mouth and Mum said: 'She always does this when we are taking her outside.' I sit here now wondering why I remember that. Even my mum remembers. Aunt Greta and Annie were in our lives a lot in the early days, so were my grandparents B——. Annie took me to the church with her nearly every Sunday and to some of the church Christmas parties, which I loved. I always got a present from Santa who was so real to me then. It was a special honour to meet him. Santa took the time to stop at Barrhead and give presents to children. For me that was magic.

Barrhead is a small town on the south-western outskirts of Glasgow, and if you stand in the middle of Barrhead on a clear sunny day, you can see the Campsie Hills near Stirling and the Barrhead Braes. This nice wee town has got some lovely green countryside around it.

I was born in a house in Main Street. Our small flat contained one bedroom and one front room with kitchen built in; the toilet was outside. We didn't have a bathroom. Instead, there was an old tin bath that we put in front of the coal fire, just like the ones in the cowboy films . . . !

Right next to oor hoose was the bakery with a small woodland area behind and we all, including my two brothers and two sisters, used to play there. My grandmother B—— (that's my mum's mum) worked in the bakers. We called her Na-Na, and grandfather was Pa-Pa for us. We used to spend Christmas and New Year together. Na-Na was a great cook. Everybody loved her dinners – you could smell them from her front gate. My mum's two brothers were always there, Uncle William and Uncle Joe. It was a great family gathering, and we always got a present each. My Pa-Pa showed me how to draw and write neatly and I loved him very much. My love for Na-Na was on and off, but today it's strong. She taught me how to be brave and tough.

My father and mother split up when we were all very little. Mum struggled with the four of us. My oldest sister was brought up by Na-Na and Pa-Pa till she was sixteen. Mum did the best she could, as my father never brought any money for us when he left. I didn't get to know my father till I grew up. My youngest sister, Natalie, was born ten years after me, when my mum married Gilbert, my stepfather, so now there were six of us. I don't remember my father in those days, only flashes of his tall, dark figure. The kids from the scheme would say to me, 'That's your dad driving past,' and I didn't know whether to believe them or not, because I really only met him when I got older.

Some memories I have of Main Street are good, others not so nice. I remember one day when I was about three years old. My brother Tylar put a Heinz Beans can on my head and told me to keep still. I did what he asked. He walked a few feet away, picked up his home-made bow and arrow and aimed at the can. I was shouting, 'No . . . !' He said, 'It's okay, I'm Robin Hood,' then fired the arrow. It hit me right between the eyes; I still have the scar to these days. All I remember of that day is screaming and running to my mum. My next misadventure was running across Main Street one bright sunny day to get a halfpenny caramel with my brother. Tylar was holding my hand. We looked up and down, then ran right into a post office van. I got the worst of it. I was knocked out, whilst Tylar had a sprained ankle. The ambulance was called and took me to the hospital. When I came round, I was all right, though I had concussion and had to rest for a few days.

We played a lot in the woods in those days; it was wonderful there. We thought we would meet the three bears, or rock-a-bye baby would fall out of a tree. We used to climb the trees and make tree dens, and it was all great fun. Sitting under a tree, I tried to imagine how lovely would it be having Red Riding Hood for a friend. I loved the grandmother in the Red Riding Hood story and always wanted to cuddle her. She reminded me of my great granny Campbell, whom we visited often in Paisley.

House at the bottom of the hill
Born by the side of a hill
it's my homeland of the poor and overspill,
the place where I belong, where passions made me strong,
through my lifetime to other intentions,
vast cities and other dimensions,
I trekked along the wayward track,
sometimes filtering my mind would go back,
and dream of when I was small,
but everything was giant and tall.
These are the reasons I'll never forget,
a wilderness of memories in our hoose was set,

sisters and brothers strong of will,
in the tranquil calmness we stand still,
the want to be wanted was our only endeavour,
the bond of our family would never sever,
for it's a magical togetherness of blood, sweat and tears,
brothers and sisters, dead or alive into the future years we strive.

T. McD. inspired by E. McD.

We were always sneaking into the back of the bakery shop to take big handfuls of soft brown sugar; this was our treat of the day. The fellow who worked there would playfully chase us away when he saw us.

Around that time Mum got offered a council house at the bottom of Barrhead; everyone called it the bottom scheme. The house was so big, it had so much space: three bedrooms with a front room and kitchen, and a bathroom with a toilet in it. What a right result we got here! No more going outside to the freezing toilet . . . There was a big piano left in one of the bedrooms and we had a great time playing any old tune but it drove our mum mad. Mum could play a little bit and sometimes she would give us a tune or two.

We didn't have a telly in those days; that was a luxury we could not afford. Most times we would use candles for light. We didn't always have enough money for the electric meter, so it was the candles. The assistance board, known as the DHSS today, didn't give my mum much money to feed us. Most of our clothes were hand downs, so we weren't beautifully dressed although we were always clean. I loved our new house. It was so roomy compared to the place we had just left.

There were lots of places to play. We used to go to the big woods which we called the jungle. Lots of us from the scheme would all charge over there most summers, and we'd stay all day. We would get turnips and potatoes from the local farm and cook them on our fire, so we didn't have to go home. I loved the jungle, it's a great memory for me. We felt free to be like the real cowboys and Indians. I really got into this game. I hated home time and if I could have slept there, I would have. I really wanted to go and live with the Native Americans.

My imagination was so alive, it could take me away from feeling hungry, as the starving feelings chased me all the time. When these feelings overpowered me, my hands would go over my mouth and I'd pretend they were a Scottish mincemeat pie, and after a while they would smell like a pie – well, so I thought. But the pains in my stomach didn't go away. Sometimes I would eat grass from the field. I saw the cows eat the grass and they weren't dead.

I would get up early in the morning, jump out of the bedroom window and go round stealing pints of milk from other people's doors. When I went on a message to the shop for my mum, I stole as many sweets as I could get into my pockets. This didn't seem wrong to me when my stomach was rumbling. I stole bottles of cheap, disgusting wine and got drunk with the older kids in our housing scheme.

One day my mum sent me on a message. I was about eight years old. On the way back I ran out on the road in front of a motor bike. It caught me on the legs, and I hit the ground. All I remember is getting up and running from one side of the road to the other. The biker was trying to ask me if I was all right, but I took to my heels, feeling a burning pain. Glancing at my knee, I saw blood gushing down my leg, coming from two deep cuts. Today's scars remind me of that. The fellow who knocked me over brought me a big bag of sweets that night. He said it was lucky he was coming up a hill, otherwise I could have been killed. This man told my mum he was really sorry. When he left, I shared the sweets with my brothers and sisters. That's a treat I'll never forget, because we didn't get a lot of sweets in those days unless I stole them. Aunt Greta said they were bad for our teeth, bad for our way of thinking. The kids in our street always had sweets, so we naturally wanted them as well.

My oldest brother, David, used to take us round knocking on doors, asking politely for any empty lemonade bottles. We got loads of bottles, then we would take them back to the shops for money in return. David would buy a loaf of bread, a pint of milk and ten Woodbine for my mum. He would get us all sweets for helping him and we would do this every week. Our friends called my brother David the BBC, meaning the Barrhead Bottle Collector. David would just laugh it off. He would say, 'At least we are helping our mum.'

My mum had a little cleaning job. She only did it to get us extra food, but some rotten swine reported her to the assistance board. Mum had to give it up sharp. Back to candlelight and cooking on the fire. It was a sin for us, that's how I saw it.

On Sundays I used to go to Aunt Greta's for dinner; it was something I looked forward to. They always had lovely posh dinners. I never ever left any food, and always cleared the plate. That pleased Aunty, because she didn't like wasting food. Aunty and Annie were good to us. After Sunday dinner Annie would fill a bag for me to take home with food that they didn't use. Mum would watch for me coming with the goodies. When I got in, we would all gather round the bag to see what was in there. That was always a happy time. Na-Na and Pa-Pa used to help in the same way when I went to visit them. I loved going home with bags of goodies; it made everyone happy.

I started to steal at the age of nine, mainly clothes and food. I had been caught by the polis, my brother David had been put in an approved school for breaking windows and my older sister was in trouble already. So, now our family had a bad name. The parents in our housing scheme shunned us. They would say to their kids, 'You're not allowed to play with that Eve McDougall. She's a bad wee lassie, she'll get you in trouble.' Or if I went to knock for my pals, their parents would tell me to my face that

I mustn't come round again. I was bad for them and always in trouble. This used to wring my guts out and bring up instant hate for those adults who made me feel like a dirty rotten germ that shouldn't be seen. All I wanted was to get out of Barrhead as far as I could. Running away was the answer for me, but the polis always caught me. In those days I wanted to grow up faster, so that I could kill the people who made me feel like a germ. I would come back to Barrhead one day and slaughter the lot of them. Those were the thoughts these people put in my head.

This made me think that I was different from other children, that I was an oddball. Everyone let me feel it with their constant snide remarks; judging me at every corner I turned. All this stuff scared me. I didn't want to grow up like those people. Who were they to judge me? Just some horrible adults.

When my mum was carrying my youngest sister, Natalie, her problems began and she had to be hospitalised for a few months. Aunt Greta offered to look after me during this time, so I moved into her flat. Lorraine, my younger sister, went to our granny B———. We were all spread out with different relatives. I started to come home late from school. This was not good for Aunty and caused her a lot of stress. One day I broke into a shop and took a big bag of money, bringing Aunty more problems when the police came to her door. They suggested that I be put in Thornliebank children's home, just till Mum got back.

I took the money for one purpose, to be sure that when my mum got out of hospital she wouldn't worry about how to feed us. I didn't break into the shop on my own, but with two other kids who were a lot older than me, as were all my friends. They looked after me instead of beating me up or making me feel odd and I was grateful for this.

The police took me to the children's home. So now I felt really deserted by all, like the bad girl; that's how the folks of Barrhead made me feel. The lady in the home took me upstairs to my new room. There were two beds, one for me and the other empty. I felt very lonely sitting on the bed, wondering what to do. I opened the window to get out. It was about two floors up but this was no trouble for me, as the drain pipe was right outside the window.

Clinging to the pipe I made my way to the bottom, then crept out of the grounds and started to walk for our hoose in Barrhead. I knew it was empty now, but where else could I go? One day Aunty's doctor had said I was too much for her: she was getting on in age and had high blood pressure. I didn't mean to cause Aunty all this trouble. Now I was sure she didn't want me. This was wrong – she just couldn't cope with me.

All my thoughts and dreams were of home and a family laugh. The few miles' walk to Barrhead seemed very long. When I got there it must have been the early hours of the morning. Knowing how to open a locked window, I went into Mum's bedroom very quietly. Thank God, I made it!

The tears started to roll and wouldn't stop. I hated that horrible empty home but what could I do about it? I just wanted my mum to be better so we could all be together again. I must have dozed off in a tearful tired state. I lay at the front of my ma's bed and thought I was dreaming when I opened my eyes to a policeman shaking me awake. He said, 'Come on, Eve, we have to take you back to the home.' I cried, 'No, please, don't take me back there. I can't stay there.' It didn't help. So we went back to the home again.

That night I did the same trip out the window and down the drain pipe and headed for my house. When I got into Ma's bedroom I slept over at the back of the bed cuddled into the wall, hoping the police wouldn't see me. To my surprise it worked. When the police came by and shone torches in the window, they missed me.

I stayed in the house for a few days till the hunger pains took over. There was no chance of going out in the daytime; it had to be dark. If the people of our street had seen me they would have phoned the police. I don't remember how long I was on the run but it seemed long enough. Turnips and potatoes from the farm were my best friends in those days. Sometimes the kids from the scheme would give me sweets and they'd never tell on me because they weren't allowed to play with me anyway.

I stole clothes and food from shops to survive. Stealing was getting easier and it was something to do. I got caught by the police again. They took me back to that nasty home and the lady gave me a right ticking off for running away. She told me to have a bath, then come back and see her – she would have my hair checked for lice. After the bath I did as she told me. Whilst checking my hair, the lady said, 'Your head is crawling and it's disgusting. You should keep it clean.' This made me feel so ashamed and dirty. I asked her, 'How can I keep my hair clean? I'm only ten.' 'That's no excuse,' was her answer. She sent me to bed.

It was still daylight so I walked out this time and headed back to our empty hoose. As I was walking along the pavement the police pulled up and tried to take me. I grabbed on to the thick wire fencing on the country road – we were by a cow field. This was a laugh. The police pulled and tugged at me; they tried everything but I wouldn't let go. I don't know where the strength came from. I was pleading with them to take me to my aunt's, so they made a deal with me. 'OK,' they said, 'after we take you to see your aunt and cousin we will take you back to the home.'

I agreed to all of this. We got to Aunt Greta's house, she let us in and the police explained the situation. I went to the toilet and locked the door saying, 'I won't come out unless Aunty lets me stay.' So the police kicked the door in. I just kept greeting, saying, 'Please, don't let them take me back there.' Aunty agreed on the condition that I behaved myself till my mum got back. Oh, I was so glad she let me stay!

Soon after this mum was home with baby Natalie, the loveliest little treasure I always wanted to look after.

My stepdad had a two-bedroom council flat out in Ferguslie Park so we all moved in there. I went to school in Paisley now, where the people were much nicer and a lot more understanding. They didn't make me feel bad. The kids were just like us. They didn't care if we had been in trouble; a lot of them had been in trouble with the law as well. The local gang was called the Young Disciples and we all used to run round shouting, 'Young Disciples rule Feagie park.' Growing up, I met the older generation of this gang. These people were all right. They didn't look upon me as a bad person for stealing food and clothes, they thought I was doing a good job of surviving. Stealing is wrong, but when you're starving it seems like a gift from heaven.

Paisley is two miles from Barrhead and is a much bigger town with lots to do. The hills and the Glenifer Braes can be seen from the Paisley cross, which was the place where the gangs used to have fights. Everyone would gather at the cross. If you were looking for someone, you'd be sure to find them there. The famous Paisley pattern comes from the weaving mills that used to operate nearby. Anyway, that all seemed so far away now. I had to be a grown-up. I was on my way to an adult prison, God help me.

Incarcerated in Prison

The police van pulled up at the prison gates. They opened and in we went. It looked like a tunnel of death. We drove a bit further to the reception door. I was wondering what the grounds looked like, as I couldn't see out of the meat wagon. The windows are dark glass and very small so one can only get glimpses of the outside. The copper rang the bell and the screw let us in. She put me in a small cupboard with a seat in it. I found out later it's called the dog box and I had to sit in there till the coppers had gone. I was taken out of the dog box, led to a big desk where all my particulars were taken, and then she said, 'Strip off all your clothes and put that white sheet round you.'

I was utterly shocked. I didn't want to do this. She told me if I didn't the officers would take my clothes off and I wouldn't like that. How right she was – I wouldn't like that, so I took my clothes off. I was riddled with shame. I felt like I had committed mass murder on the people of Barrhead, not broken into a shop. It was so degrading. When the screw pulled the sheet away she started looking round my body to see if I had anything on me. I felt sick. I was ordered into a bath – the warmest pal I had found yet. It was all a nightmare and I couldn't wake up. Bathing was a quick procedure as you weren't allowed to lie and soak. There was no shampoo. I had to wash my hair with Derbac soap.

One of the cons gave me a set of prison clothes – the prison uniform. It was unbelievable: nylon stockings with rips, a women's roll-on with suspenders to hold them up, knickers that were cheap brushed nylon and were stained at the gusset. They had been worn by the whole jail by the looks of them. I complained but I was told very sharply, 'This is a prison, not an approved school. If you do crimes, you have to do the time. There are a lot of rules in prison.' I said, 'Yes, and I shouldn't be in a bloody jail and made to live under rules for women over 21 years old.' She said I would have to talk to the Guv'nor if I had any complaints. I did and a few weeks later the Guv announced that we were being issued with three pairs of cotton briefs each, which was great.

This prison was very eerie. It had a feeling of hundreds of ghosts that were still in prison even though they were dead. I felt a lot of pain just looking at this place. I still can't remember going from the reception area through to the big hall. I remember a long corridor, then the gates into the hall. I stepped in and the screw locked the gate behind her. Everywhere I went the doors were unlocked and locked. It was scary. The main hall is massive, with four floors. All of the floors to my knowledge were just cells. I was led to a cell on the ground floor, one of the observation cells. The constant banging and jingling of keys hit me. Everything was banging and crashing – doors, gates. It did my brain in from that day onwards. I wrote this in memory:

Thinking back

I'll never forget this pain,
no matter how I try.
for every time I try to,
it makes me feel the same pain
over and over again . . .

Sitting in this prison cell,
staring at the walls
I feel so sad and lonely,
For the freedom my heart recalls.

Being caged all day long,
it seemed to me so very wrong.
no one to talk to, no one to tell.
Oh God! This is hell.

All you hear –
footsteps
on the floor,
with no face.
Jingling keys,
banging doors
all day long
just that song.
Please, NO MORE!

They put me in the cell and the door was shut. At least I was alone but not sure what to do. I lay on the bed and stared round at my new home: a table and chair, a small wardrobe, a chamber pot for doing the toilet in, also a wash hand basin. The walls were a nasty yellow gloss with the wee bricks staring through the paint and there was a small barred window. *'That little tent of blue that we prisoners call the sky.'* (Oscar Wilde)

In a cell

There is not much to tell
in a cell
staring at the ceiling,
lazing on the floor,
looking at the door,
hoping to wake up
and this cell will be no more.

Walking up and down,
sitting, looking round
can't hear a soft sound,
in this clouded vision
that I have found.

Thinking of home
and a family laugh,
never dreaming I would
end up in this gaff!
No one to talk to,
nothing to do.
I just sit here feeling blue.

As I say,
not much to tell
incarcerated in this cell.
There is a safety bell
on the wall,
alas no one can hear my call.

A frantic and desperate
look at the door,
an empty hope this cell
will be no more.

The tea lady was the next person I saw. At about eight that night the door was unlocked. So-called supper time! There was a cup of tea with something in it and a slice of bread with margarine. It was nice to see someone as I thought they had forgotten about me. I was disgusted when I tasted the tea and asked the tea lady, 'What the hell is in there?' 'Bromide,' she said. 'It's to stop the women from getting sexual feelings.' Oh, yeah! Now I was really thinking that these people were trying to kill me.

Dear God! Help me! The night went weird. I tried to be tough but tears fell down my face. Being in a turmoil I dozed off and woke up suddenly to the banging and crashing of doors, gates, jingling keys. This is bloody murder, how can we keep sane when all this disturbance is fired into our brain daily?

My cell door opened. The screw showed me where to slop out the chamber pot. I didn't use it. I swore to myself that I would never bloody use it! It was disgusting to me, that piss pot. Honestly, I got so constipated at times just because of my horror of shitting in it and having to sleep with the smell of it all night.

The toilet was an open archway; it had two toilets, two sinks and a sluice where we emptied our dirty water. We had to wash our bodies in a wash hand basin every night and every morning. We would go to the arch, fill our basin with water and take it back to the cell where we could wash in privacy. It was very sad. I would wash my face first, then under my arms. I had to think what to wash first: my bum or my feet – it was all very disgusting, this procedure. The biggest laugh was when we had to wash our bra and pants in the same water. This was the filthiest rule I had come across yet. Also, the inmates were only allowed one bath a week and one clean towel.

This rule has really stuck in my mind as my mum always said there's no need for filth when there is plenty of water. Mum taught us cleanliness all our young lives. She was always cleaning the hoose and I'm just the same.

In the next cell to me there was a fourteen year old, who had been there a few weeks. I wasn't allowed to talk to her or anyone else till I had seen the Governor – another rule. The rules were never-ending. While I was waiting to see the Governor, the breakfast arrived. I was told I would always eat in my cell as I wasn't allowed to mix with the women at any time. I thought it was a bloody joke. I had already spoken to about seven women. I talked to them through the wee hatch on the cell door. When the women brought the tea round they said it was a tragedy putting children in prison.

Oh, the breakfast was like the shit pan … rotten! The porridge – just thin, tasteless hot water, the toast – cold, like stone, the tea – with bromide in it. There was a bit of so-called bacon – as hard as a rock. All of the food was on a steel tray, which made it taste of metal. This first day I couldn't eat anything, still trying to get into my thick skull that this was a prison. I even asked the screw why the cutlery was plastic and she explained, 'Well, you won't injure yourself or others.' Was this another joke? I was wondering why anyone would want to do that. I didn't have to wonder for too long: this place was enough to drive a dumb animal to injure itself!

Measuring this cell step by step, up, down, then around, ranting and raving. Caged in this room with no one to talk to and no one to tell ... It's branded in my head that this is a place for the living dead.

The door opened, and I stepped out. As the officer locked my door, I noticed a card on it with my name, my age, and C.Y.P. There was a number on the card as well. This number was my new name. The officer said, 'That's what you are now – a number.' I was taken to see the doctor and he started to ask if my general health was all right. I said, 'Yes.' 'Are you on any medication?' I said, 'Naw ... ' I felt like saying, 'By the time I get out of here, I'm going to need bundles of medication.' The nurse was next. She checked my hair for bugs and told me I would be seeing a gynaecologist to have a smear test just in case I had a disease or an infection. I nearly fainted. I told her she couldn't make me do that, she would have to get my mum's permission. She just laughed at me saying, 'The officers will hold you down.'

I thought it was the end for me now! I had never had a smear test or sexual intercourse, so why didn't they just leave me alone? The nurse told me I would get this test done in a few weeks. That was a weight off my mind for now. This smear business scared the hell out of me. When I saw the Governor I told her my fears about getting this test. Being very sympathetic she told me to read the rule book carefully. 'If you didn't obey the rules,' she said, 'you would be put on report.' I couldn't take all this about the C.Y.P. sentence into my brain in spite of all the Governor's explanations and efforts to help me. I was still in shock after being sent to jail. All I could think about now was dying in this cold, horrible hole with all of these cold, horrible people. The Governor was saying, 'You are allowed one letter a week so you will be issued a letter today.' I was taken back to my cell and given a sheet of paper. Writing to my mum I told her everything that was happening so far. When the door opened for lunch I gave the screw my letter and asked her why I had to stay in the cell all day. She said, 'We don't have enough officers to look after children like you, but don't worry, you'll be allocated to a place of work soon.' How long was soon, I wondered . . .

It was time for lunch, which looked like pig slop. I ate the potatoes and the turnip – they were my favourites – but I couldn't eat any more. To my horror I started to greet like a big baby, crying into the pillow so the screws couldn't hear me. This was all my own fault. If I hadn't been drunk I wouldn't be here. I asked myself if alcohol was a problem for me and rather than admit it I put it out of my mind. It must have been about an hour later when the door was opened and I was taken to the far end of the hall where two gates led out to the exercise yard. Outside all the women were walking round in pairs in a big circle with a few screws scattered around the yard. I had to walk on my own with a screw (another prison rule). I had a sad, lonely, broken feeling that gave me a pain in my chest that wouldn't go away.

After walking round for an hour in the freezing cold we had to go back to the cells. When I was walking back the principal officer pulled me into the office and told me to rewrite my letter. I couldn't understand why and she replied, 'It is against the prison rules to write about the prison in letters and if you do it again you will be put on report.' I asked her if it was all right to breathe.

I was locked up in my cell thinking, 'I've lived under much fear in my life and now I'm being put to the full test with horrible thoughts of death.' Dying seemed like the only way out of there.

The light and the dark of it,
the cold wind that blows around it,
the rules and regulations of it,
the fear of it – Gateside prison.

These adults didn't have a clue what all this was doing to my mind. I flopped down on the bed feeling very angry. A tear rolled down my cheek, then another. The tears flowed silently for some time. Suddenly the key went into the lock. I jumped up and sat at the table – otherwise I would be put on report for lying down.

O well for him whose will is strong,
he suffers, but he will not suffer long,
he suffers, but he cannot suffer wrong.

Tennyson

Forget the hours of thy distress,
but never forget what they taught thee.

Gessner

The Guv'nor informed me that I would be allowed out to watch the telly but I had to be in thirty days before this could happen (more rules). I was being treated the same as the women cons, and this left me feeling confused. My brain felt very disordered and tired. These rules and regulations were very threatening. How would I live through this punishment? I just didn't know . . .

This poem tells you a bit about how my head felt then.

Headflows

Headflows in my brain,
the silent one, who kept me sane,
the monsters cried out to be free, from me.
I couldn't let them
I couldn't let them
destroy me
When the evil burst from my stem,
no control did I have then,
deep darkness swallowed up my mind,
the silent one I couldn't find.
I couldn't let them
I couldn't let them
destroy me.
Battling around in my lonely soul,
I loved alone on my fearless ground,
I couldn't hear a soft sound.
I couldn't let them
I couldn't let them
destroy me.
Prison took my young life
to a place of dark doom,
where my evil monsters could roam aroon.
I didn't want this
I didn't want this
to destroy me.
People feared me,
some did love me,
But not too many had the energy.
I wanted love

I wanted love
Will it destroy me?
The evil craved my soul,
love broke it on a whole,
the heartache wouldn't go,
What did the silent one know?
Stormy headflows
stormy headflows
wouldn't let go.
Mentally I could go anywhere,
bodily I was stuck,
with this grime and muck,
The silent one was struck.
Prison's luck
prison's luck
won't destroy me.
In my sadness I write this poem
of a devil, a monster,
a silent, sane person.
This I want to be known
that I am all of these alone.
Stormy headflows
in my brain
Stormy headflows
kept me sane.
God said do not hurt my little children.

I hope you can see through my poem how inside out I felt. Oh God! Why am I in this sty? The court date was getting closer – 22nd December 1972; three days before Christmas. It was a chilling feeling. My birth date seemed to fit in with this situation. Was I this much of a fool? The three-week remand had been torture and I wasn't allowed a work place. Remand prisoners are locked up twenty-three hours a day with one hour exercise (if the weather is good). To get a work place you have to be convicted. If I had been allowed to talk to people it wouldn't have been so bad. These punishments freaked me right out: 'Don't talk to this one,' 'Don't talk to that one,' 'You can't do this,' and 'You can't do that.' Whilst asking an officer if I could go to the toilet she shouted, 'We don't have time to take you, we look after women – not children! Use your chamber pot.' Well, I was sick; I couldn't use that thing. I held it back and got bad constipation pains.

It felt like my head was crammed with punishment. There was no room left in it for soft thoughts. Those thoughts died the day they put me in jail. It was the 21st of December. By this time my nerves were wrecked. I actually thought the judge would see what a silly crime this was. Maybe they would let me go with a fine to pay for the broken glass on the baker's shop door. This was the most foolish thought. I was in for a shock. I didn't sleep a wink that night. It was murder – tossing, turning, getting up, pacing the cell with a glimmer of hope that I would be set free . . . Surely they would see that being hungry and only fifteen doesn't mean I should be sent to prison.

The dawn finally came, the keys started to jingle, time to get up . . . After the women slopped out I was taken to slop out. I was always taken out after the women as I wasn't allowed to mix with them. Breakfast went very quickly, then I was taken back to the reception and put into the dog box. The screw told me to strip off the prison clothes, then she gave me a clean white sheet, telling me to step over to the next dog box where my own clothes were waiting. I was ordered to get dressed . . . the police van would be here soon to take me to court. I felt glad to be getting out of here even if it was only for a few hours. A day at court was like Christmas. Although I had feelings of being freed, there was a wee voice in the back of my mind saying, 'You're not getting out, McDougall . . . ! You're coming back to jail.'

The reception bell rang; this must be the police van. The screw let me out and handed me over to the policewoman. We got into the van and this felt better than being locked away with no one to talk to. I got glimpses of the countryside as we headed for the Paisley Sheriff Court. It was so nice to look outside, so peaceful. I wished I was a bit of mud or a strand of grass – anything was better than being locked in jail! The journey seemed so quick to the courthouse and before I knew it I was being locked in the court cells. How I loathed these peters, they were so deadly . . . I had just put out a roll-up when the polis opened the door and said, 'You're up in the dock, McDougall!' My heart felt like it was punching me in the chest, I was so nervous. Knowing that my ma would be there was of great comfort to me. When I walked into the courtroom there she was, sitting in the front. We sort of smiled as our eyes met but it wasn't a very confident smile. We both knew that the social worker, this horrible Miss Cool, had put the worst report in. So, Ma's look said a lot to me then; I was definitely going back to jail. I stepped into the dock and was told to sit. The clerk said, 'All rise!' when the judge entered, and we all stood up. The judge sat down, then the people did the same. My crime was read out along with the social work report. The judge who read it looked at the report, then at me, saying, 'Your social worker thinks that you are unruly and out of control. I am sending you to Gateside prison on a C.Y.P.' He read from the Social Work (Scotland) Act 1968:

Any court, on remanding or committing for trial a child who is not liberated on bail shall, instead of committing him or her to prison, commit her to the local authority in whose area the court is situated to be detained in a place of safety chosen by the local authority for the period for which he or she is remanded or until he/she is liberated in due course of law. Provided that in the case of a child over fourteen years of age it shall not be obligatory on the court so to commit him/her if the court certifies that he/she is of so unruly a character that he/she cannot safely be so committed, or that he/she is of so depraved a character that he/she is not a fit person to be detained.

Where a child charged summarily before the sheriff with an offence pleads guilty to, or is found guilty of, that offence the sheriff may order the child to be committed for such period not exceeding two years as may be specified in order to such a place as the Secretary of State may direct for the purpose of undergoing residential training, and where such an order is made the child shall during that period be liable to be detained in that place subject to such conditions as the Secretary of State may direct.

A child detained pursuant to the directions of the Secretary of State under this section shall, while so detained, be deemed to be in legal custody.

Any child so detained as aforesaid may at any time be released conditionally or unconditionally by the Secretary of State, and any such child conditionally released shall be liable to recall on the directions of the Secretary of State and if he fails to comply with any condition of his/her release he/she may be apprehended without warrant and taken to the place from which he/she was released.

How was I supposed to understand this? All I could take in was the words 'two years'. Was it a bad dream? *Two years* for being starving? No . . . ! No . . . ! It couldn't possibly be! I wanted to shout out, 'You're wrong, you're all bloody wrong . . . !' Mum shouted out, 'This is ridiculous, she's only fifteen! You can't do this!' But again, they did ... As I was being led away I glanced at Ma's face, trying to smile at her bravely, saying, 'Don't worry,

I'll be all right.' She looked so torn and broken. The copper took me down to the cells. I lit a roll-up and dragged on it heavily, thinking, 'This is not real! It's a nightmare –I'll wake up soon.' But this was real and I had to wake up fast, being incarcerated in an over-twenty-ones' prison for the second time now. How sad!

Let me tell you . . . I'm in a right state of confusion. How can a courtroom full of educated people lock a child up in a prison for such a silly crime? Miss Cool must have really convinced these people of the law that I was worse than a killer. On the way back to the dreaded Gateside I didn't say goodbye to Paisley. This time I was in a right state of shock.

The trip back to Gateside prison seemed to be over very quickly, and my brain was still numb as we drove up to jail for the second time. After handing my papers to the gate screw we headed for the reception. I didn't speak a word to anyone after we had left Paisley Sheriff Court. There were no words to say, no words of comfort, *no nothing* . . .

The police van pulled up at the reception, the copper took me to the door. When the screw opened it and saw me she asked, 'What happened?' 'Well, I'm not so sure,' I said, 'but it looks like I've got two years.' Looking at the copper she commented, 'This is a tragedy, this girl is only fifteen.' The copper made a nasty remark, saying, 'She shouldn't have broken the law.' What a cold poliswoman!

I was put through the reception quicker this time. After all, I had only left that morning. All I wanted to do now was lie down on the bed and greet my eyes out. The screw took me back to the same cell and locked the door. The tears poured from my eyes like a river. I just wanted to go home to my mum's and have a nice cup of her tea.

That night the office was empty; the screws had gone for tea break. I heard a small voice saying, 'Hello, what is your name?' I went to the wee hatch. It was the fourteen year old in the next cell. We told each other our names, then shared our crimes. Chris told me there was a fifteen year old in the Young Offenders, the next hall to us. The Young Offenders was separated by a locked door. Chris said she had been in a boys' school before coming here. I got to know the girl from the Y.O. later. I find this sad to write but that girl killed herself when she got to her late twenties. God bless her soul and keep her safe. I understand how she must have been feeling.

I would talk to my new pal next door whenever the coast was clear. Chris told me that she was supposed to be sent to an approved school but I didn't know what was going to happen to me till I had seen the Governor.

I tossed and turned all night. No matter how much I tried to sleep, I couldn't. I wanted answers to my questions, for instance: *What does C.Y.P. mean? How long am I to be kept in jail? What about the two years? Why haven't I got a release date?* All sorts of questions prevented me from sleeping. I was in agony. Morning finally came round. This was a relief, knowing I would see the Governor soon and get all this confusion sorted out in my head. Feeling like an old woman I crawled out of the bed; my body ached all over with the stress of it all. The 'banging doors, jingling keys' operation started – the screws were in. The questions spinning round in my head would soon be answered when I saw the Guv'nor. Waiting to see this Governor was like waiting to be sentenced all over again. I felt sick. Time to slop out, then have breakfast. After breakfast (if you could call it that) I got washed, dressed, and was waiting patiently to see the Governor. The time was just dragging.

A few hours later the cell door opened, I stood up and the screw told me I would be seeing the Governor, then the doctor. I was taken to the Guv's office and she started to answer my questions. I still couldn't come to terms with this jail. The Governor was very nice to me; she tried to help me to understand the law of it. She said I could get out in under a year if I behaved myself. None of this was a comfort to me. I was getting very depressed sitting in that cell with no one to talk to. She told me I would be going to work in the sewing room the next day. This was a bombshell. I loathed sewing and told the Governor this. Well, these are the rules, you must obey them or be put on report. I didn't want to be locked up in my cell for twenty-three hours a day with one hour's exercise and loss of all privileges.

This place was a constant punishment. The Guv also told me I would be going over to the Borstal when I turned sixteen. This training could be done in seven months or anything up to two years, depending on one's behaviour.

My birthday wasn't till April. I was sent to jail in December but after my birthday I had to wait another month before I got sent over to the Borstal. All these laws were freaking me out. It was against the law to put me there at fifteen although it wasn't against the law to put me in an over-twenty-ones' prison. How am I supposed to understand this? Would it not be more reasonable to put me with girls near my own age rather than keep me with adult convicts where there is a greater chance of corrupting my young mind?

After I saw the Guv, I was informed I would need to see the doctor to get a smear test done. Oh no! This is right out of order! Can they do this to me?

A screw took me along to the sewing room and handed me over to the officer in charge, Miss Birch. She led me to a big table with a sewing machine on it. There were rows and rows of machines and a big table in the middle for cutting out material. The noise was well rowdy; it was hard to think – I couldn't even hear my thoughts. Oh, God! What punishment is this? Then the civilian officer, Mrs Heel, came over. She lived up to her name. Mrs Heel was a very cold woman but I must admit she was a good teacher. This woman didn't like it when I lit a fag up in her sewing room at tea break. She ran at me and slapped the fag right out of my hand. 'You hit me!' I screamed. The women were saying she had no right to touch me, I was only fifteen. They suggested that I tell my family. We were supposed to work till lunch time without a fag – it was a rule. This wasn't justice, that Mrs Heel and the officer were allowed to smoke while these poor women couldn't. After she slapped the fag out of my hand I was marched back to my cell and put on report to see the Governor next morning. I told her the truth – I was gasping for a fag. 'O.K., you will spend the rest of the day locked up.' Nothing was mentioned about Heel hitting me. Oh, you just can't get any justice in this place.

Back to the sewing room next day. When I walked in it was tea break and all the women clapped when they saw me, saying, 'Look, we're allowed to smoke at tea break, thanks to you Eve.' They gave me fags and biscuits. I started to laugh and laugh. Mrs Heel hated me now and life in the sewing room was so boring. I couldn't take much more of this. Jail was pulling me down and I was getting scared of my thoughts – I wanted to die. We were getting so-called wages for working in the sewing room and they were (have a guess!) twenty one and half pence a week. What could I buy with this money? A half-ounce of Golden Virginia, one small packet of rolling papers – and the wages were gone. I had to scrounge matches from the women, which they gave me without hesitation. With a dressmaking pin one could double the matches by splitting them in two or three – a handy wee procedure.

The women were all whispering in a huddle. I wondered, 'What's going on?' Apparently there was a thirteen year old coming in for murder. My God, she must be a right hard bitch! I didn't know much about it. You see, we were not allowed newspapers. The ones the women got had bits cut out of them and the bit about the thirteen year old had been cut out as well. Every few days when the women had read the papers someone would slip one through the wee hatch on my door. Sleeping at night became very difficult for me – all this shouting and banging! Some of these people should have been in hospital – not prison. One Indian woman who was supposed to have killed her baby would howl for hours on end every night. The women would tell her to shut the f . . k up but naw, she wouldn't give up. More crap was being fed into my brain, and it was not good for me.

I had sent my mum a few passes and told her what was going on but there was nothing she could do about it. This broke my heart, to drag her up here to listen to me moan. I decided not to send any more passes to Ma, give her a break. When I got a visit I wanted to leave with my mum because it upset me too much.

A screw called me out of work to get the smear test done. I protested to the nurse, saying, 'I'm only fifteen, this is out of order.' She just asked, 'Shall I call the officers?' I got up on the chair with the stirrups, she did the test and I felt as if I had been raped. This whole situation was so dirty, so horrible . . .

I put my things back on and the screw returned me to work. That's when I saw the thirteen year old. She was a thin rake, looked like she couldn't kill a fly. I was told not to talk to her or ask her what she was in for – we already knew what the crime was. Giving her another glance I noticed that she had very twitchy eyes and was very nervous. This I could understand. I felt nervous all the time. I wondered why she took a life. What made her kill?

A screw took me back to work and I sat myself down at the sewing machine. That horrible smear test had left me feeling sick and disgusted with adults. I had just been raped by the prison authorities. All I could see was that heartless woman's head in between my legs with a long stick in her hand, then those scary stirrups. I wondered if the electric chair looked like this chair – a big black monster that was going to eat you up.

Miss Birch asked me if I was all right. I told her I felt sick and faint, so she sent for an officer to take me to the cell. Back at the main hall they asked me again how I felt. Instead of answering I ran for the archway and vomited all over the place. One of the screws told the Guv'nor and she said I was allowed to lie down for the afternoon.

I flopped onto the bed, the door was locked, and they were gone. I cried myself to sleep, feeling wounded by these spineless people who were so threatened that if we didn't do as they said we would be put on report instantly. The year of 1972 was coming to an end, and another two fifteen year old children came in. There were now six of us under the age of sixteen years all in Gateside prison. When I went back to work the next day the women were asking me how I felt. I told them the truth, that I felt as if I had been raped. When they heard this, they all looked at me with tears in their eyes. Their reaction gave me a lump in my throat. But this didn't last long: Heel shouted, 'Come on ladies, I don't see you working.' What can I say? We don't get time to sympathise with each other in jail, the rules don't allow it, so we all got on with our work.

My eyes opened to the wee bricks . . .

God, it's Christmas Day and I feel so lonely being cut off from my family and friends at this festive time of the year. It seemed so wrong and cruel to me. The whole jail got the day off work at Christmas and on Boxing Day. A radio was playing in a distant cell and the sound of Christmas carols made me feel really sad and homesick. After breakfast everyone gathered in the bottom of the main hall, the record player was brought out and we could play the records all day. We only had to be locked up for an hour so that the officers could have their Christmas dinner.

I got talking to everyone freely all day. It was great just to mix with the others. Being with the people helped me a lot. Even if they didn't talk to me, a smile was a good treat for my soul. But we did talk. We talked a lot, mostly about Christmas dinner – it was the highlight of the day. This would be the first time they allowed me to eat with the others. The mere thought of having dinner with the cons really excited and overwhelmed me. I could hardly wait.

Finally, the time came. We were all told to line up, and the screws led us to the church, where Christmas dinner was served. It felt good – to sit and eat, to chat to all the different people. It didn't matter what they were in here for, the women were really nice to me and that was more important.

During the course of dinner the women had a sing song. Some would do their party song, say a poem or tell a joke. It was brilliant and a good laugh. At the end of the day I started to feel like I was finally thawing out from the shock of being incarcerated. One of the women shouted out, 'You sing, Eve.' 'God,' I thought, 'what will I sing?' Everyone was saying, 'Come on, sing!' Standing up and feeling very nervous I started to sing Chuck Berry's song *My Ding a Ling*. Well, the whole jail joined in on the chorus; the place was rocking by the end of the song. I got a big cheer from the women and the officers too. Great feelings passed through me. So many times in my life I had been told that I only made people sad. But now I could see I had just made a lot of people happy.

The women gave me back some faith in the human race. I didn't feel so alone now. The New Year came. This was the same as Christmas – we got the day off and had dinner in the church. I sang *My Ding a Ling* again to another big uproar and lots of clapping, which made me feel special again. I got a natural buzz from that song. Thanks to Chuck Berry for bringing such happiness to all of us cons. After New Year I and the other youngsters were told we would be getting educational classes. This freaked me right out as I was useless at school work. I went to classes with the others. The schoolteacher's name was Miss Alexandra Kirkpatrick. I found her to be a great teacher and a really nice, understanding woman

– she knew I didn't like school work.

I would do my best, and even though that was useless, Alexandra always encouraged me to draw, paint and write. She liked my essays and said I could be a writer one day. Thinking back on those words helped me write this book. We would have our classes on certain days but we still had to go to work. I despised the sewing room then. I wanted to stay at classes with Alexandra. She made me feel safe which gave me some strength to carry on in this God-forsaken place.

Thirty days passed and I was allowed out for association, which meant we could watch telly or play records for two hours each night or we could go to classes some nights. I chose to go to pottery one night a week with some of the women. Walking into the pottery class was a bit of a shock. The teacher was from my old high school. Mr Balfour said, 'What are you doing in a prison, Eve?' I told him about my foolish crime, and he said, 'My God.' I said, 'We mustn't say any more. If the screws hear me talk like this to you I'll get put on report. Mr Balfour would have lost his job too. I never spoke to him about it again. I wasn't much good in the pottery class – I just couldn't concentrate. I found it hard to do anything, always having a feeling that the law had ripped me off from my young life.

The other youngsters and myself were all allowed to mix now. We had a laugh and would imitate some of the officers and their ways that were funny – how they walked, talked to us – but mainly we watched telly or played records.

Borstal

It was now May 1973, and it was time for me to be shipped over to the Borstal wing. This was good news for me, at last to mix with people my own age and get out of this jail. The thirteen year old who had done the murder was being shipped out too. She was not going to Borstal; she got sent to a place for kids with special needs. I saw the injustice in that but, please believe me, it wasn't envy, although maybe a little jealousy. I wished her luck and didn't want her to feel the way I was beginning to feel about prison, no matter what she had done.

I shouted to God, 'Where the hell are you? These prison judges don't know their ass from their elbow. I said my farewells to the young ones and the women.

I said goodbye to the officers that didn't have an attitude problem. Big Miss Robertson, she gave me a bear hug. She was like a big sister to all the young ones. She could make you smile even when you didn't want to. Wee Miss Henderson told me to be good. I would miss her. She used to let us watch the dog show on a Sunday and she wasn't supposed to. The Matron also said farewell. She had always been nice to me and had a warm smile.

I arrived in the Borstal a few seconds later, as it was all in the same grounds. There were a few people in Borstal that I knew and we started the Borstal training together. Training went like this: first you had to work hard, be on your best behaviour and scrub a lot of floors, then you would get a stripe. Yes, just like in the army, if you kept all this up you got a collar which meant you were on your way out. It sounds easy but when you are under pressure it's not easy.

I didn't get a good feeling in this Borstal. The screws were right cheeky hard bitches; the matron, Mrs Shewit, was the worst. Her nickname was Hatchet because when she shouted she came down on you like a hatchet breaking logs.

Part of the training was scrubbing the big long hallways. I still have a bad knee and sore hands from those hallways. When the matron came into the hall in the morning we would look up and she would shout at us, 'This is not a holiday camp – get your heads down and scrub.' Honestly, these screws were a right bunch of rats. What sort of attitude was this? It didn't matter what I did, they all showed bad attitudes towards me, saying, 'You're not over in the jail now. We're not going to pet you like the women and officers did.' I didn't give a damn what they did; I just wanted them to leave me alone. It was tough enough without them taunting me. Borstal was all head games. This disturbed me very much and made it feel as if it was a war zone and not a Borstal. If I get pushed too far, someone will end up getting hurt. The screws won't get a look in if they drive me to play head games. I was taught head games by the best. The women warned me about the Borstal and gave me some useful advice.

The Borstal routine was very boring and went like this. When our doors opened in the morning we headed for the arches. This time we could stand and wash at the sinks and we were allowed two baths a week. In the jail you only got one bath a week because there were more inmates there than there were in the Borstal. Three men officers worked in the Borstal, which I didn't fully agree with. There was Mr Smith who would stand in the hall; he would watch the girls go to the wash room. He was supposed to stand in the office when the girls got washed, but not him – he always stood in the hall looking at us. We girls thought he was a pervert. We complained about him staring at our bodies in the mornings. He was told not to stand in the hall when we were washing. Mr Shaw was all right. He taught us to play the guitar. He was a really laid back fellow and didn't act like a screw. The third screw, Mr McConnell, who reminded me of my dad, was really laid back and treated us all like the girls from St Trinians. A few of the women screws were okay: Mrs Rollo, wee Maw O'Brian, along with a few others.

As I said before, part of our routine was scrubbing the hall from morning till lunchtime. After lunch the scrubbing continued on the upstairs landing, then we had to clean the sitting room and make tea for the officers. What they got in their tea I cannot say. If the screws were rotten to us their tea got done.

I was working with a pal called Lynn. Lynn is a twin and her sister Susan was my best pal. I stayed at Lynn's mum's for a while before I got sent to jail. Lynn's parents were really nice people and her brothers were like brothers to me. Her mother would always be singing in the kitchen and cleaning her house till it shone like the sun. Her dad would be whistling and dancing in the front room. We had a laugh at Susan and Lynn's house. Susan's boyfriend Jack would come round and we would all go to the Paisley cross to see if there were any gang fights going. Let me say there was never a dull moment at Susan's house. Lynn, myself and our pals did the best we could to get through this Borstal training. I met lots of girls; some of them were okay, others had problems. I met an Irish girl. She was just sixteen years old, the same age as myself. I got on really well with Carrol and also her pal Mag. These two girls were a right scream; they should have been on telly.

A few months had passed since coming over to the Borstal and I was set up for a fight with another girl who ate needles. She should have been in hospital. I walked into the archway and the girl attacked me, trying to pull me down by the hair. I stuck the heid on her and held her by the hair. This was stupid and she was ill. The screws ran in and pulled us apart. We were carted off to our cells where we were put on report. It was bloody silly. How could I hit someone who ate needles and slashed her wrists? This poor soul had scars from the wrists to her elbows. She had scars all over her legs too. I got put in my cell for three days; so did she. After the three days in our room were up, I met the girl in the archway at washing time. We looked at each other and laughed. It was never brought up between us again.

I had been in a jail with all adults and my outlook was different from that of the girls. I had to adjust to their way. It all started to disorder my head even more.

I couldn't get over the amount of people who had slashed their wrists, legs, necks and bodies. Some other girl had actually stuck pins in her knees; she did this just to get to hospital for a few hours. People would do anything to get out of this hell hole. The poor souls should have been in hospital, not jails and Borstals. The lassie inmate who ate the needles was given bread and cotton wool to eat; this procedure helped bring the needles out in her shit. I am crying my eyes out as I write this. It was all very sad. Why wouldn't someone get these lassies out of here? They were in for petty crimes, not murder.

We all used to gather in the sitting room. Mr Shaw would get us playing the guitars and we would sing along with him. He loved the Beatles' music so we all did eventually.

Mr McConnell would tell us mad jokes to keep our morale up. I really liked those two – as screws go they were all right. Mr McConnell left to go and work in Barlinnie men's prison. I was sad when he went, one more half-decent screw had gone. After he left he came back for a visit to see us all. When he was saying goodbye the tears rolled down my cheeks. I was pulled into the Guv'nor's office and asked if I had a crush on Mr McConnell. When this was put to me I felt sick and humiliated. The man was like a dad to us all.

I looked the Governor straight in the eye and told her he was like a dad, not someone I had a crush on. She said that she believed me, which I was glad of. I found out later that one of the screws had planted such a thought into the Guv'nor's head. The screw was a rotten witch for insinuating such nonsense.

I saw Mr McConnell a few years later when visiting my ex-husband in Barlinnie prison. Mr McConnell was on the visits. He came over to both of us and we all had a chat about the Borstal. I never saw him again.

It was hard trying to get the white collar and I didn't get it. The screws weren't happy with my disordered head that they had created. I thought, 'Right, I've got to get this collar and leave this war zone,' but these screws were playing head games with me. Okay, let's play head games. I didn't want this. It could all get very nasty. They would never let me forget I was in Borstal now. I sometimes wished to be back over in the prison. Why didn't these Borstal screws grow up?

I was sitting in my cell trying to play the guitar, thinking, 'These screws ought to lighten up or there will be a bloody riot.' I did cause a riot. It freaked the screws and the Governor right out. I won't go into detail about this riot but it stopped the head games and the snide remarks. I wouldn't want the young ones out there to think that jail and Borstal were glamorous or all riots. As I said before, it was a nightmare that I haven't forgotten and never will.

My brother Tylar came up to the Borstal to see me a few times. If it wasn't for him coming to see me, how would I have got through it? I looked forward to those visits; we would have a right laugh. The girls would shout to him, 'Can we go out with you?' He just laughed. Tylar would tell me all about the latest films that he'd seen recently. This was good as it gave me things to think about. Tylar also gave me strength to go on. Thanks, Tylar. I would have been allowed to go out with my brother for a few hours but due to the riot this was not possible.

A disordered one

A disordered one is what I've got,
a personality that I didn't plot,
I'm a fifteen year old con in a jail,
the disordered one was born.

I learnt it in our daily routine,

listening to the cons, dream after dream,
all the violent scenes,
screws dragging cons to the padded cell,
cons shouting and screaming.
Don't hit me, leave me alone.

Never allowed to read a newspaper,
always kept in the past,
sleeping in this horrible prison,
where I've grown a deathly mask.
It's called jail pallor where we all look the same.
Nothing to lose, nothing to gain.

I learnt a lot of wrong from the women,
but you see – it's not their fault.
It's all a game to keep the brain sane.
Never-ending lies, untold tales,
mostly from the ones waiting on bail.
The lifers and long-termers said nothing.
Ye' see they knew that the years ahead
were no bluffing.
And after all that,
I'm still working hard,
with my disordered personality,
that's split me apart.
So I work on it night and day,
hoping it will go away.

Thinking back on my teenage days there is not much to remember, as institutions had been my life since I was nine years old. Now, at only sixteen, it wasn't looking good for me. Borstal had this eerie bad vibe. It was like an evil invisible demon; one could only feel it. My thinking was beginning to swing – I was nice to people, then nasty to them. Some of the lassies pointed this out to me at a meeting one night. I looked at them all and said, 'If I've been cheeky to you, I'm sorry,' which shocked the girls and surprised the screws. I had been a bit of a cheeky bitch but only because of the mood swings.

This feeling of being at war with myself was very depressing, conflict upon conflict. It was murder in fact. The need to direct my confusion somewhere was very strong. I blamed the justice system, the prison authorities. Who else could I blame? It certainly wasn't my doing.

Was this the guinea pig way, to see if putting kids in prison would work? Oh yes, it worked fine didn't it? Look at the state of my head. I'm all mucked up and I wish to God I was dead. What sort of training is this?

I had seen a psychologist a few times in the prison and was asked if I wanted to see her again. This was okay with me. She was nice and I liked her very much. Erica was her name. She would come to the Borstal and do group meetings; also visualisations. The relaxation helped keep me sane. It was a new, nice feeling.

The battle with my emotions hurt my head. I got headaches through this. It was no use telling anyone. That would do no good. One had to have one foot in the grave before you could see a doctor in here. I charged on and did my best to keep my heid straight which was very difficult for me.

I told one of the principal officers I wanted to join the army on being released from the Borstal. She put me on a right downer, saying that I wanted to join the army because I was institutionalised. I don't think she was being horrible. She was trying to point out that I could be addicted to these institutions. This didn't help me. It felt like I had no say in my life any more. If I wanted to do something, the officers would put me off by saying this wasn't good for me or that wasn't a good idea.

I gave up saying anything. That's what happens when people don't hear you. I withdrew and went right into myself, which is not good. It made me feel poisoned. Seemed everything I thought up was a bad idea. The screws made me feel like I was no good. My social worker, Miss Cool, said she would get me a job in a sewing machine factory all because Mrs Heel from the prison said I was good at using a sewing machine. Can you imagine how I felt when the Guv'nor told me this? How can they just do what they like with me? I told her straight I didn't want this.

It didn't matter how I felt. They had it all planned already.

I sat in my cell playing the guitar, thinking they can all go to bloody hell and back. They didn't have to go far. How dare they send me to work in a sewing machine factory when I had told them very clearly sewing wasn't for me. Honestly, sewing machines were my enemy. Mrs Heel put me off them for life. Part of the Borstal training was working in the sewing room. That's where I was working now. I disliked it so much it started to get confusing for me. I was making a pinafore but I couldn't work out how to do the simple bit of putting the bib part on.

I understand now that it was the disordered one creeping up on me when people wouldn't listen to me. All the confusion built up anger in me, then utter bloody hate. I thought my heid would blow up at any time. I was beginning to feel like a walking bomb.

When these terrible angry thoughts went flying through my mind the silent one couldn't be found. Banging and battering my head off the walls till it felt numb, then lying on the floor staring at the sky, made me feel better in some strange way. I would go round for the next few weeks feeling very light-headed. Every few months we would get bouts of depression. This happened to everyone – it's called the jail blues.

It's very heavy on the human brain. You can't explain to people what's happening to you. It's really the circumstances that we were living under at the time. Being locked away from the world, living under constant threat, the never-ending rules and head games.

Not everyone banged their heids off cell walls – well, not that I know of. One night when the moon was shining bright. I started to bang my heid off the wall. The night patrol man must have seen me and got on to the night screw through his radio. The screw was at my door asking me if there was anything wrong. I told her I was okay.

In the Borstal the windows were different from the ones in the prison. They were bigger, with clear glass. The bars were on the outside and you could open the window about three inches at the top but not the bottom.

Some of the training in Borstal was in the form of classes. They were as follows:

Laundry training

Sewing

Cookhouse

Knitting

Cleaning/Scrubbing

Educational classes

Miscellaneous (e.g. community work).

We had to work in these jobs for a few weeks at a time to get to the next stage of the training. If the screws weren't happy with us, we would do extra weeks of training. This was always the case with me. I never got through anything in one go. The screws couldn't fault my work but they didn't like my attitude. But they had created this attitude, so what didn't they like? I think I was a mirror reflection of their own attitudes.

They basically wanted me to grovel to them. No chance. I will get through this. It took me a lot longer than others to get to my collar.

There was an extension on the back of the Borstal. It was called the Annexe and it had about ten cells, a kitchen, a sitting room, a shower room with bath and a classroom too. This was for girls who had just about done their time. It was great. We didn't have screws breathing down our necks all the time. They only came by to check that we were okay. It was much more relaxed.

Home

The time came for me to get out. They released me at the end of February, 1974. I had been here since 1972. I was glad to be leaving, although a sad, doomed feeling still roamed the pathways of my soul. This was due to the fact that I wasn't allowed to choose my job. What chance did I have? The social worker and the prison authorities had seen to that. The night before I left the Borstal the girls sang the farewell song. This was sung to everyone before they left. The last verse of the song goes like this:

You're about to cross over this Borstal line,
the waiting is over, it's the end of your time,
you're now one step closer and it's heaven divine,
you're about to cross over this Borstal line.

I couldn't believe it was nearly all over and I got out of bed before anyone else. While we had breakfast my thoughts were of the freedom I recalled. I still had the feeling of doom in my gut. I really wanted to be joining the army, not going to work in a sewing machine factory. The noise of sewing machines made me feel very disordered. What could I do? Nothing. It felt like the end and not a new beginning.

I didn't want to go back to the life I lived before but what choice was there for me?

On the train home to Paisley my thoughts were in a right turmoil. I wasn't happy and it should have been a happy day for me. More disorder poured through my soul like an evil whip. I felt as if it was lashing out just at me. I wasn't used to all the people – it was manic to my ears and very scary. Anyway, walking round to the bus stop at the Paisley cross, realising I had been away so long I didn't know how much the bus fare was, I found myself running over the road through the Paisley cross and towards the East End where my mum lived now. I chapped the door and she opened it and said, 'Oh, Eve! You're out of that terrible place.' She gave me a hug. Mum had some tea ready and we sat down together. She said, 'How did you get home?' as she hadn't seen me get off the bus. I told her it was all too much for me. She laughed. How could she understand? I told her about the job and she said, 'It's bloody ridiculous. You should have a choice in your own future.' But I had no choice in my future at this stage. Mum said I must at least try to work in the sewing machine factory. It felt very strange sitting drinking tea with my ma. I was in a state of shock trying to take in freedom. Freedom to walk to the toilet without asking. Most of all freedom to talk to whom I pleased.

It was off to the factory for McDougall in the morning. Mum told me how much the bus fare was. When I walked in, all the girls stared at me as if I was a killer or something very dangerous. Tea break came and I sat on my own. The girls stared at me. One girl came over and tried to be nice to me, saying, 'What were you in Gateside for?' This shocked me. I said, 'Who told you that?' She said, 'Your social worker told our boss that we should all know where you have come from.' This put the icing on the cake. The disordered brain I had inherited in Gateside blew a fuse. Swiftly and quietly I walked out of the factory. One of the girls came after me, saying, 'Don't go. You'll get sacked.' I said, 'Fine,' and kept on walking again. I ran home to my mum's.

She opened the door and saw the mixture of hurt and pain on my face. She got some tea and said, 'Tell me what's wrong.' I told her that all the girls knew where I had come from. Mum said it was confidential information that should not have been told to the girls in the factory. She was horrified; she felt the humiliation I was feeling. I went to look for my own job and found one in an office. It was better than the factory. At least the people here didn't know I had been in jail and it was peaceful – no roaring, noisy sewing machines.

I had been out a few weeks and found it difficult to get on with my life. Jail had done a lot of damage to my brain. I found it very difficult to communicate with people, like a loner. My insides felt so poisoned by the rules and regulations, the injustices, that I had seen in jail. One dark night while I was standing at the chippie with some mates, eating chips and chatting, one of my friends said, 'Watch out, Eve, that lassie is going to beat you up.' I said, 'For what? I've done nothing to her.' Just at that moment this tall lassie was in front of me saying, 'Think you're hard, McDougall, just because you were in a jail?' Then she pushed me to get me out of her way. My disordered brain snapped. I attacked her as she attacked me, battering her to the ground. I stopped and looked at her and thought, 'What am I doing?' I told her never to underestimate people smaller than herself. What had just happened was horrible. Being in jail at my age you had to put up with a lot of contenders. People were always looking for a name, but they weren't going to get it through me after what I *suffered* in jail. No one was going to push me around any more.

The lassie had me lifted by the polis. As I walked away from her, someone shouted, 'Polis.' The chase was on. I looked round and the copper was running after me. I took to my heels and ran like the wind, but I didn't run fast enough. He caught me and dragged me back to the meat wagon, then chucked me into the back of the van and slammed the doors shut. We headed for Mill St police station. The copper said to me, 'You're a bad wee bastard. You have really made a mess of that lassie's face. She is charging you.' It didn't matter what I said to him – he wasn't going to believe me. I had just come out of Borstal and jail. I had no chance.

Set Up

We got into the polis station and I was handed over to the C.I.D. They took me upstairs to their office and asked me what my side of the story was. I gave them my version and told them to ask my mates, so they did. I was charged and let go to appear at court. When we got to the court I was found not guilty of assaulting this lassie. I walked out of the Paisley Sheriff Court for the first time ever. My mum couldn't believe it. We looked at each other very cautiously. This was a fix. Something didn't smell right – like a rat. My social worker, Cool, walked over and said, 'I would like you to come and see me early this week.' I went to see her once a week; this wasn't my choice, it was a rule. I looked at my mum and said, 'What is that dirty scum bag up to now?'

I went to the social workers' office and had that terrible feeling of doom come over me again. This social worker couldn't stand me; she hated me. I've stated her hate for me many times in this book. My mum said I should have had another social worker, as this one obviously didn't like me. I told the receptionist I was here to see Miss Cool and she said to take a seat. Cool calls me in to her office. I nearly died when I walked in and saw the big polis woman sitting there. This was a set up. DAMN YOU, MISS COOL, DAMN YOU TO BLOODY HELL. I didn't say this to her; it was all in my head. My soul was silently crying out to God, 'Please Lord, why have you let them do this to me?' Miss Cool was delighted at the shock on my face. She was even more turned on when she said to me, 'You're going back to jail.' Cool waited for my expression. Before I could give her a look, the big police woman spoke. She said, 'Eve, I don't think it's right. This is not my doing.'

I was so glad the big polis said that to me. I needed something to feed my brain at that lethal moment in time. The big polis woman was my saviour – also Miss Cool's.

Miss Cool said, 'Right, off we go ... back to Gateside prison.' She had joy on her face. She said it with a big smile. The big polis woman looked at me in horror. Cool's heartless attitude towards me was unreal. It was difficult to take it in. Cool put me in the back of the car handcuffed to the copper. The big polis gave me a fag to smoke. Thanking her I said, 'How can she do this to me?' She said, 'It's the C.Y.P. Act. You can be taken back to jail without a hearing.' She was very sympathetic towards me. The polis kept saying, 'It's not right to put you back in that prison.' I don't remember the poliswoman's name. But thanks for the fags you gave me and for showing me your feelings. That meant a lot to me. It saved me from killing Cool. If the big polis hadn't butted in when she did, I don't know what I would have done to Cool. The big polis saw something that was so wrong. I did too. But Cool was in her glory. She didn't think she was in the wrong, Miss Cool. I forgive her for what she did to me. I need not slay slayers, for their time will come. I have found this be true. I have paid for all my crimes, even the ones that were only a thought in my head, I can assure you. You are about to read more of how I was slain by human laws.

I had not been allowed to contact my family from Cool's office. She said I could write a letter from jail to let them know. My thoughts then went like this. Cool was a thoughtless, very cold, heartless woman who was there for the money. Cool didn't give a damn for a young human life that she was destroying. I knew I was going back to that cold, windy Gateside on the hill. These were my inward thoughts at the time.

Jesus on the cross,
please don't let me get lost.
What have I done that I must pay this cost?
Is it for wanting revenge on some people
who treated me like a monster

when I was little?
Or is it because I defended myself
at the chippie that night?
Oh Jesus Christ,
don't take away my young life!

We were driving up the big hill to the jail. The big polis gave me my last fag. I told her I wasn't looking forward to this. She said, 'It's all wrong, Eve; I don't agree with this.' Cool pretended not to hear us talking. We pulled up at the jail and the screw booked us in at the gate. Off we went to the prison block. Cool rang the bell. An officer opened the door, looked at me and said, 'Back so soon?' I had only been out about two months. My face had no expression by now. The injustice was so clear. I could do nothing of my own self. I hadn't even asked how long I was back for this time. I couldn't be bothered to talk to Cool after the dirty rotten stroke she had just pulled on me. God forgive her. Does she know what's she's done?

She looked at me before leaving, saying, 'Maybe you'll learn how to behave yourself.' I wouldn't look at her. I ignored her and said to the officer, 'Shall I wait in the dog box?' The screw said, 'No, Eve, you can get straight into the bath after I search you. Cool turned to the big polis and left. I knew then Cool was out of my life once and for all. Cool was the worst example of a social worker that had ever been shown to me. She had no compassion whatsoever.

I was kitted out with the prison uniform. The wrapover dress, the roll-on with nylon stockings, the winkle-picker shoes that crippled my feet. Then a screw took me through to the main hall. I was in complete shock, with the sickest feeling inside. By now it felt like I had never been out. This was the end for me now. I was only a few months into my seventeenth year on this earth and back in jail. This prison was so hard, so cruel for the soul, one had to be brave – very brave. I felt sick and just wanted to lie down and cry my eyes out.

I walked to the office to get checked in and the principal officer, Miss Mckinnon, said, 'This is terrible, Eve. You shouldn't be in here again. It's not right. Jail can do a lot of damage to your young mind.' She told me I would see the Guv'nor in the morning and that in the meantime I would have to be locked up for the rest of the night. I could only say to her, 'Miss, do you know how long I will be here this time?' She looked at me sadly and said, 'I don't know, Eve. Ask the Guv'nor in the morning.' Oh God, I don't know what is to become of me but don't let this destroy me, whatever happens.

This time my cell was on the first floor with the remand prisoners. The ground level had observation cells and the top two floors were for long-termers. I waited for the tea with bromide in it and a piece of bread and margarine. Nothing had changed. I heard the jingling keys and banging doors. I knew the tea was on its way. At last the door opened. The big officer, Miss Robertson, said to me, 'Eve . . . this is terrible that you've been put back in here.' 'Tell me about it,' I said. Then wee Miss Downie came along. She said, 'It's cruel. You shouldn't be in here.' At least this made me feel sane again. Other people could see the injustice. All of these people can't be wrong, can they?

I undressed and got into the bright blue brushed-nylon nightie. This made me itch so much, I would wake up in the middle of the night and take it off. I got the pillow and the blankets, put them all in a big ball and started to punch into the bed, saying f . . k them all. I could see Cool's face and I punched till I could punch no more, then paced the cell saying this:

Gateside, you have every inch of me,
Gateside, you've split me like lightning strikes a tree.

I would sing it to myself in my cell. They had my body but sure weren't going to get my mind. I had to protect what was left of my brain and get through this somehow. I thought, 'If this is what growing up is like, I don't want to grow up. It would be better if I were dead. No justice – 'no one to hear me crying, only the dark and the dying'. My brother Tylar wrote me those words in a poem. They feel so real to me, as they do to him.

The morning came slowly. I didn't sleep well; it was a restless night. All my thoughts were of injustice. All night that word haunted me. The banging gates told me the officers had arrived. It would soon be time to slop out our piss pot, then get water to wash in. Breakfast on that steel tray with our plastic knife and fork, the plastic spoon for our watery porridge. Not forgetting the brick hard toast with bromide tea. I still had to eat alone in my cell. I was too young to mix with hardened cons – the same procedure as before. I had to wait thirty days before I could associate with the six other girls that were under sixteen. I was the only one who was seventeen years old.

The trip to the doctor and nurse were still to come. This scared the hell out of me. The last visit was still clear in my mind. The day they gave me that horrible test was a brutal blow. My fear of seeing the nurse was terrible. I thought, 'If anyone touches me again they'll get knocked right out.'

A screw took me to see the Guv'nor and the Matron, Mrs Last. They said it wasn't right that I had been brought back to prison. I agreed with them. But there was nothing they could do. The Secretary of State and the social work department had control of what was to be done with me. Nobody could help me. Doomed again. I asked the Guv'nor how long I would be here this time. It was up to the Secretary of State was her answer. Aye, they could keep me for as long as they wanted. It felt so dead, just like before. As if I had done a murder. This treatment was so insane – it was twisting and scrambling my brain.

I asked the Governor about the smear test. She said, 'Don't worry, you won't have to go through that again.' This was a great relief, thanks to the Guv. I also asked if I would have to wait the thirty days to get out to association. She said I could get out to gather with the other youngsters in a few days. I didn't have to wait the long, treacherous thirty days and nights.

The Guv'nor also said I could go to work the next day. This was good news as long as it wasn't the sewing room. Reading my thoughts she said, 'Don't worry, you will be going to work in the women's laundry.' She also stressed, as she did before, that I must not talk to the women. This was impossible. Working alongside them how could I not talk to them? The women were all saying, 'It's a bloody tragedy that you're back in jail.' Aye, they were right – it was a bloody tragedy, but the Secretary of State didn't seem to think so. I am back in hell.

When I walked into the laundry it was a shock for the officer, Miss McDonald. She couldn't get over the fact that I was in jail again. The women I worked with were really sympathetic and gave me roll-ups. One woman I got on very well with was big Sadie. She gave me a Mars bar. For someone to give you a Mars bar in jail was a big thing. A Mars was like gold – a right treat. I never forgot big Sadie for that gesture.

It was a right laugh working in the laundry. Miss McDonald was funny; she never bothered us. As long as the work got done, Big McDonald was happy with us. The laundry was a door away from the Borstal and we did some of its laundry. This meant I got to see some of the lassies that had been old friends. The first time I took the laundry off the girls and I said to them, 'How ye' doing?' they didn't get to answer. The Borstal screw said, 'Don't you talk to the girls, McDougall. You're in prison now, so don't forget it.' I was ashamed of that screw for talking like that. A lot of the Borstal screws smirked at me when they saw me back in jail. I could feel their dislike for me – see how they wished me ill-luck. I forgive these people for the way they treated me. After that I never spoke to the lassies again. Smiling at each other we would make faces behind the screws' backs. We would pass notes to each other when we could.

One night we were all going to our cells. This screw said to me, 'Into your cell!' I replied, 'Don't panic, I'm going.' She said to me, 'You little tramp.' I turned round, walked over to her and spat right in her face. Then I said, 'Don't you ever call me a tramp, screw.'

Well that was it: report for McDougall. I knew exactly what to do. I walked right into my cell and kicked the door shut and sat on the chair. I knew she was running to get the P.O. and some more officers. They all came charging up to my cell like a herd of cattle. The P.O., Miss McKinnon, came in first. She said, 'That is the filthiest thing you've done to my officer. You're on report.' I said, 'I know.' Miss McKinnon was telling me to say I was sorry. I said nothing. If I had flinched or made the slightest move the screws would have grabbed me and taken me to the padded cell with the two doors. They would have stripped my clothes off, then put a straightjacket on me. I had seen it done to other women. They would get the male screws from the gate to help out when this sort of thing happened. I found it very disturbing when I saw these things. I got very scared. It looked like rape when they cut or tore the clothes from the women. For a male screw to help on those occasions was very scary. I wasn't going to let that happen to me, no way. I've had enough of this prison pain. I mentioned the little hatches that were on the cell doors when I was on the ground floor the first time I was in this jail. When the women were being dragged down the stairs to go to the padded cell, I could get my head out and see exactly what was going on. It all terrified me the first time. Now, when I heard it, it just became a part of this prison life. When a woman was being dragged down, all the other prisoners would shout, 'Ya' bastards, leave her alone!' Nothing could be done. One of the worst things about jail was the on-the-spot cell searches. Two screws would come in and search your cell from top to bottom. I had to strip all my clothes off and the two screws would look you over to see if you had anything you shouldn't have. This was rape again. Where did it all stop?

There were a good few fights in prison. The child killers got some stick. I saw a woman throw a basin of scalding water over a baby killer. I turned away and sat in my cell. You could hear her scream like a pig. I kicked the cell door shut, saying, 'Oh God, please let me out of this hell hole.' There was a great tension in the jail. Everyone was like a bomb waiting to be triggered off. It's a lot of stress. I got scared of what I would be like when I finally got out of there. Jesus, don't forsake me. Please don't let me spend the rest of my life in and out of jail. I'll die, bloody die. Please, Lord, hear me.

I was taken to the Guv'nor the next morning and she read out the screw's report. The screw denied calling me a tramp. I gave my side of the story. They didn't believe me. I was doomed. The Guv'nor said it was disgusting, spitting on one of her officers. She told me to say sorry. I told her there was no justice; I wouldn't say sorry. So I was locked up for twelve days' punishment. I said 'This is okay.' I think they thought Eve would crack up at this. The tension in the Guv'nor's office was very heavy – three screws, a P.O., two governors, all waiting to drag me to the padded cell. I showed no signs of cracking and told the Guv'nor the screw was a liar. But I wasn't heard. They were only concerned about the poor officer.

I started my punishment 23 hours a day in the cell. The mattress was taken out so that the punishment didn't give you any comfort at all. I was allowed to read Mills and Boon love stories – very educating. The screw I spat on came to take me to the library to get some more sick books to fill up my head with far-fetched love stories.

When we got into the library I said sorry to her. Only because I knew I would get days off my punishment – one of the screws had told me so. I forgot to tell you that one week was put on to my sentence whatever that was. I still didn't have a release date. After I said sorry to the screw I got out of my punishment early. I was getting very fed up with the rules and regulations of this jail. I felt like dying every day. Why didn't God take my life away? Heaven has got to be better than this. Some days when I wake up now that I'm free I still get the feeling of dying, for no reason. I think I should be dead. I want to find that place called heaven. This prison carries out a lot of the devil's work. It's hell.

I had been brought in here in the summer time. It was now winter and cold, draughty Gateside would howl when that biting wind blew around it.

The most depressing thing about being on the remand landing was watching people coming and going. Some would go to court and not come back. Others would be in and out like yo-yos for petty crimes. I didn't bother to make friends – it only got upsetting. You learn not to get close to people. The only people I ever got close to were the girls in the Borstal. I wasn't allowed to talk to them now. I was in prison and it was against the rules for me to talk to people. I only ever spoke with the children who were sixteen or under. Our conversation was limited. I was now seventeen years old. I had the disordered head of a forty year old woman – well, that's how it felt. I saw so clearly that the injustices of this jail were all wrong. I still couldn't believe I had been brought back here without a court hearing. I felt like a wild animal inside, eating out my own guts with pure confusion. I couldn't accept it. I felt constant rage in the pit of my soul.

Like I said, it was coming up to Christmas, 1974. This brought back memories of my last two Christmases spent in jail and Borstal. I'll never forget the Borstal Christmas Day. I drank a tin of Brasso polish. I was so depressed I downed the lot, then felt really sick and ill. That was the only escape from these walls: a few hours of feeling ill. What a buzz. The last time I drank Brasso had been in the jail in 1972. I saw one of the women do it and asked her what she was drinking. She said, 'Brasso – it gives you a good buzz.' So mug here tried it. Oh aye, it was a buzz all right. A banging headache and an upset stomach. When I burped it sounded like an old rusty pipe. I thought I was floating and I laid down on my bed. That was the buzz. This was very common in jail. There wasn't any other escape unless you made a deal for valium. Some of the women would do a deal with their valium for tobacco or a Mars bar. When I think of it now, I laugh a sad laugh, seeing young people addicted to these pills and many other drugs.

I feel that locking humans up for 23 hours a day disorders the brain and makes it vegetate, especially in children who can't understand prison. I saw people – calm people – turn into raging lions. These people left prison with a right chip on their shoulder, another personality disorder. These poor souls would be in and out of jail often. I know how they felt. I was one of them.

> Ye' cannae buy two lives
> Ye' can buy two bags o' crisps
> But ye' cannae buy two lives
>
> E.McD

One of the things that sticks out clear in my mind about jail is the amount of people who slashed their wrists and throats. Some people also ate knitting needles broken into bits and even dressmaking pins. This scared me. What if I did the same? But I thought, 'No, I'm too brave.'

I'm not sure of the release date I was given. December 1974, before Christmas. This was good news – to be out for the season's greetings. The time now was even slower than usual. Every second would seem like an hour; the days and nights would just drag by.

Everyone saw the Guv'nor before leaving the prison. This was a rule, the Guv'nor told me. I didn't have to see a social worker any more, which was a great relief. I would have asked to see another social worker anyway. I couldn't have taken another dose of that dragon Miss Cool or stood in the woman's company again. Cool was a very bad, brutal example of a social worker. All social workers are not like she was. I think they have a very difficult job.

Again my nerves got the better of me, waiting to get out of this hell hole. I couldn't sleep. It was always like this. No matter how many times you go in and out of jail, it's still nerve-racking. The last night feels like the whole sentence over again. Time in jail goes very slowly.

Battered Wife

When I got out, I went to live with my older sister in Barrhead. It was the worst mistake I ever made in my life. I could still feel bad vibes from some of the people of Barrhead. People whispering behind my back. I met a bloke and got married to him in the February of 1975. Ian Islip. Everyone had warned me about this man. I didn't listen. People told me he would batter me and give me a life of misery. He had already beaten his mother up a few times. He beat his brother, his sisters; their lives were a living hell. The day we got married he punched and kicked my body all over for no reason. He got drunk and I was his personal punch bag now. Well, I had been warned this was a madman.

When he woke up the next morning, he couldn't remember anything. I forgave him. I thought marriage would be like the Mills and Boon marriages, ha ha. I was in for the biggest shock of my life yet. I had come out of jail, got married and fallen from the frying pan into the burning fire. The Guv'nor had told me if I ever needed help just to call her at the prison, and if she wasn't there, to leave a message. I nearly called her up the day after I got married. But I would make a go of this rotten situation I had got myself into now.

I spent the next months as Ian Islip's punch and kick bag. He would torture me beyond all reason. Every single day this man would hit me. If he got up in a bad mood, that was it. I was done for if his tea didn't taste right. He would chuck it at me or bounce it off the wall. I was black and blue most of the time and mentally done in. Death was my warmest thought.

Islip's treatment was killing me. Was I paying for every fight, every argument, everything I'd ever stolen? Islip was my payment. I strongly believe that is true. I know what it feels like to be severely battered. The mental torture was agony. Islip wouldn't let me go anywhere without him. He was always there. It was like a very slow death. After he battered me I would go to the toilet – to be alone, away from him. The toilet was my sanctuary. That soon stopped. He started coming to the toilet with me and he would stand there watching me. It was humiliating, degrading. He was like a screw and I was back in hell.

One night I had an argument with his youngest sister. I told her to shut up and leave me alone. She knew my life was hell. She waited till my husband came in and told him what I had said to her. I nearly died when she did this. I didn't think she would want to see me get the shit kicked out of me Well, how wrong I was. She showed me how much she hated me.

Islip got me by the hair and gave me full force punches into my stomach, face and body, shouting at me, 'How dare you threaten my baby sister.' He then said to his sister, 'Watch this.' He grabbed me by the hair again, then literally threw me down a flight of stairs, saying, 'Die, ya' bastard, coz' if you don't die I'll fuckin' kill you.' I was pregnant when Islip put me down the stairs. He knew this, so did his sister. They didn't care. I was lying at the bottom of the stairs thinking, 'I have got to get away from this bastard. I can't fight this monster. Oh God, what is to become of my unborn child? I've got to get away – get my baby to a safe place.'

I couldn't go to my mum's. He only found me. When he did find us he battered us in front of my mum. He pulled my hair to the ground and booted me in the face repeatedly till blood was dripping from it. If I didn't have black eyes he would punch and punch till they were black. He dragged me home on the bus. A bloke from school said hello to me. Islip accused me of chatting the guy up. He threw me to the floor punching and kicking me, shouting, 'Whore! Whore!' He loved that word. This was on the bus in front of the fellow. Islip called his mum and sisters whores for years before he met me. Now he had us – his unborn child another one of his victims. At least his family would get a break from him now.

My heart really felt for my husband's sisters and brother. He had tortured them for years – and many others. His mum had to jail him because he beat her so badly. The only time they were happy was when he was locked up. Islip was a jailbird and that is what attracted me to him in the first place. I also was a jailbird.

Islip would stop me from visiting my family. He would keep us both in the house for days. He would say to me, 'You're a useless dirty whore – you should be dead. He would say my time would soon be up. He would go on like this for hours on end. If I started to doze off, he would batter me all round the room till the blood was pouring from me.

I had enough one night when he was battering me. I went to the toilet to be sick. The baby couldn't take these beatings much longer. I sort of fainted. This wasn't the time to faint. I was too scared to faint. I pulled myself up and knelt over the toilet pan and threw up. Islip came into the toilet. He said, 'Stop being sick,' and punched me right in the face. I felt my teeth crunch. Oh no, my teeth! Can't worry about that now – I must get out. When he left the toilet I got out of the window, then ran two miles to my mum's. She would cry when she saw me.

Mum always got me some tea. She would tell me to phone up the psychologist – Erica, the one I had met in prison. I had attended her clinic at Charing Cross, Glasgow. I went to the clinic a few times after I got out of jail. I didn't have to go; it was optional. I had got to like Erica very much. She was like a sister. I told my mum I would phone Erica. I didn't phone her for a few weeks. Islip had promised to get help – go and see a counsellor. He did go to see a counsellor and the batterings stopped. Not for long: he soon got fed up with the counsellor. Instead he got back into battering me and our unborn child.

Like I said, my mum always cried when she saw my constantly battered and bruised face and body. Why didn't I leave? Everyone smirked at me. Why did I always go back? Did I love this monster? No, I was infatuated. No one could love that. Now I pity the people around him. I had nowhere to run to any more. I had hidden in places but he always found me. Someone was always ready to tell him where I was. I called such a person a sewer rat. I stopped running to my mum and my friends; it was bringing my grief to their houses. My mum didn't complain but I knew it was hard for her. I stopped running. It was beginning to look like I'd never have control of my own life.

Battered

Blood all over the place,
horror and dread,
at the state of this creature's head,
he's so mucked up, he's got to be fed.
Fed with violence of a psychopathic kind,
he doesn't care what he's done to my mind.

A Wicked Fist

There is an almighty crash,
as I feel my body get kicked
and bashed.
The boots into my guts
are so very harsh.

I get the razor blade
so now I'm slain,
I've cut my arms to bits
and I can see
through the clear slits.
I've got no places
left to go,
or anyone
who wants to know.

So, my cut and painful arms
wouldn't bring me any charms.
For me all this – just a nightmare,
and everyone would stop and stare.

But when they saw my scarred arms,
I could see their red alarms
of mortal horror and blatant shock
of a battered body that could still walk.

E.McD.

I didn't know what to do when he battered me. My head was all over the place. I even thought I would be better off in jail. I tried to fight back but it was useless.

One night he walked in through the front door and kicked me

right in the lower abdomen. I was about four months pregnant. I fell to the floor and jumped up. I ran for the toilet, then threw up. Islip was shouting, 'Stop pretending to be sick, ya' bastard.' As I said earlier, he had started to come to the toilet with me. I got constipated. How could I pee or do the other with this madman watching me? He thought I would jump out of the toilet window. The torture he was putting me through was beyond all reason. I couldn't reason with this beast. I had to get to safety or this baby would not survive.

I contacted the prison to speak to the Governor, Martha Bruce. I explained to her that he was battering me, and that I had slashed my wrists. She was very sad and concerned for the baby and myself. She was so concerned that she herself and the Assistant Governor, Agnes Curran, came from the prison in Greenock to my house in Barrhead to help me.

When they arrived at my house I wasn't there. The neighbours told me two social workers had been looking for me. I knew it was Martha Bruce and Agnes Curran, and I phoned them back. We made plans to get me out. I had Islip arrested for trying to kill me. He stabbed me with my own razor blade. I was really terrified of this guy now. I hoped he would get put in prison.

It had got to the point where I would slash myself, so that I would get taken to hospital just to get away from him. He soon put a stop to that. He refused to phone an ambulance when I cut myself. He would batter me when the blood was pouring from my arms. Oh God help me. I can't let this monster kill me. I thought, 'If anyone is going to take my life, my all, then it will be myself.' The McDougall clan war cry is 'Buaidh no Bas', which means 'Victory or death'. I understood this and wasn't prepared to let Islip take my life.

It got so bad one night, I was screaming and crying out to the neighbours, 'Please get the polis,' but they were too afraid of what Islip would do to them. I threatened to cut him up if he hit me one more time.

I had two razor blades, one in each hand. He was coming at me and I couldn't do it. What if I killed him? I couldn't do the life sentence that would follow. He started kicking and punching me and I forgot about the razor blades. Then he grabbed my hands from behind me. We both fell and the razor blade cut the side of my pregnant stomach. I was lucky it wasn't deep. This wasn't real! I couldn't take any more. It was every day that he was battering me. There was a knock at the front door! It was my big sister; she talked her way in. I ran over to her, but Islip said, 'This is none of your business. Get out of my house.' My sister pleaded with him to get me an ambulance. The blood was dripping down my side and arms. Islip put my sister out of the house and she went to get my big brother, Tylar. A wee while later there was another knock at the door. By this time Islip was kicking me round the front room like a ball. He told me to keep my mouth shut or I would die.

Islip opened the door a wee bit and a big axe smashed into the wood. My sister had told my brother that Islip was going to tie me to the rail track behind our house. He had told her he would kill me. Islip shouted at me to get the police to have my brother Tylar arrested. I laughed and ran for the back door of the house, while Islip was trying to hold the front door shut. My brother Tylar was trying to get in. He thought Islip had killed me. Six police officers pulled up and were knocking at the front door. Tylar took to his heels when he saw the polis motor drive up.

Islip opened the door to the polis. I came in from the back garden and said, 'He's trying to kill me.' The police told Islip they were arresting him and they took him by the arms out of the front door. Islip tried to get away. It took six polis to handcuff him, then get him into the polis van. Watching them drive away was a relief. The police got the ambulance and I went to hospital where I was safe. I had charged Islip a few times for battering me. He always talked me out of it with promises that he wouldn't do it again. So mug here would drop the charges. I left the hospital and went back to the house of horror and cleaned up some of the blood. Then slumping to the floor I cried my eyes out for hours and hours. I was so glad the torture was over. Carolyn and Anne came round that morning. They were shocked at the amount of blood in the house. These two girls were my friends. They were even more shocked at the state of me and asked how I had survived such an attack. I told them it was like *The Exorcist*.

Martha Bruce set it up for me to go and live in the country where my baby would be safe. She took me to a house run by a charity set up for families who can't get a holiday, which is great. The drive to the big house in the countryside was like a dream for me. I was getting away from the house of horror. The house Martha Bruce took me to was near Stirling and was called Braendam.

Braendam

We drove up to the very posh-looking house. I thought, 'Gosh, this has to be a lovely dream.' A tall lady appeared at the front door and introduced herself to me, saying, 'I'm Lilias Graham.' I shook her outstretched hand. It was a nice firm hand; it made me feel safe. I thanked Martha for helping me. I was very grateful for her help. Martha was a very busy lady but she said she would drop by when she could.

Lilias showed me round the house and introduced me to the housekeeper, Kathleen. These people were all so nice. Lilias took me to my room. 'Yes,' I thought, 'I'm safe from the beast.' I'll never forget the help Lilias gave to me. I loved this big house. It was a dream, walking in the fields, tramping the woods without fear of Islip. Thank God Martha knew Lilias.

The time came for me to have my baby. I went to hospital a few days before my time. The big house Braendam is situated between Thornhill and Callender, a good few miles away from Stirling Royal Hospital. Away I go to have my baby. I was terrified. It was so scary to have a baby. The nurse took me into the labour ward and put me on a drip to bring on labour. The pains were coming but the baby wasn't. The doctor asked if I would like an epidural. He said this would numb the pain. 'Yes,' said I. This epidural was not working on me very well. Maybe it was because I was scared. Anyway the hours went past. The pain was bad but there was still no sign of the baby. I was feeling there was something wrong when the doctor came in and looked at me again. He said, 'I'm going to put a needle into the baby's head to take some blood.' This was very uncomfortable. It was painful. I was terrified again. The doctor took the blood sample away. Then he came back; he wanted another blood sample from the baby's head. No way! I couldn't let him – it was too painful. He went away. I was in a right state of terror, scared stiff. All the fear I felt from Islip was coming back to me. Oh God, take my life, spare my child.

The doctor came back and told me to prepare for an operation. My pelvis was too small and this meant that the baby's head would be crushed. I was taken straight to the theatre.

I didn't recover from the operation very well. I woke up in the intensive care ward the next day. I asked for my baby and the nurse brought her along. All I could do was stare at this wee baby. She was so lovely. I started to cry. I couldn't take it all in. It was a miracle she had survived Islip's abuse.

The first person to come and see me was my brother David. We just sat staring at my baby girl. Big D. was saying, 'What does it feel like to have a wee baby?' I said jokingly, 'Bloody well sore.' Both of us laughed. The next person to come was Martha. She brought some clothes for the baby. She had knitted them; they were lovely. Alexandra came to see me and she gave Jackson, my daughter, a present. This was so real. Kathleen the housekeeper came to see me. Lilias came with a Japanese girl who also worked at the house – Chyoko Gyhitchi (I think I've spelled her second name right). I loved all these people. They had all been very kind to me and now they were all here to see me.

I went back to Braendam House with my new baby. I called her Jackson McD. Islip.

A few weeks later I went back to Barrhead to Islip. He promised he would never hit me again. I wanted it to work. I was so very wrong. He started to beat me again and when I threatened to leave him he would say, 'Jackson stays but you can go.'

One night my mum came to see me. Islip got drunk and started to beat me up. I ran out of the house away to my brother Tylar's and phoned Braendam. They said they would take me back. I had to go back to Islip to get Jackson. I stayed again. This running away became a habit. I phoned Erica and she took me to her own home to stay. She clothed me and fed me. She was really kind to me. I'll never forget this, although I went back to him.

More Abuse

The final blow came when Islip started to batter me and rape me. This went on for a few days. My face and body were battered beyond recognition and I slashed my wrists again. He wouldn't get me an ambulance. Islip warned me not to tell anyone or he would murder me. He said it was his marital right to take me when he pleased. My brain was dead and my heart felt like it was dragging behind me. I really wanted to kill this monster. He went out to get bottles of Eldorado wine. While he was gone I packed some bits under the mattress in Jackson's pram. Her wee clothes. I knew he would get drunk, beat me up, then rape me again.

Then, after that, he would fall asleep. I decided that the monster was going to die. I couldn't run out while he was at the off licence because he ran there and back. I couldn't go to the one bus stop; he only caught me. I was sick of running. He had been sleeping with girls in our town and would brag to me. He even showed me the sheets they had slept in. He told me this always happened when I'd left him. No way was he going to get away with any more of this. I had decided that he was going to die.

I had just fed Jackson when he came back from the shop. My mum turned up and Islip was getting drunk and threatening to drop the baby on the kitchen floor. The floor was stone. My Mum talked him out of it. I put Jackson in the pram.

Islip started to drink some more. He pretended to fall asleep. Mum left, saying, 'If he starts battering you, phone Erica.' I promised her I would. Meantime Islip got up and tried to hit me. He missed. He was too drunk. I guided him to the bed, giving him the wine. He drank like a pig, dropped the bottle and fell asleep. I picked up the large scissors lying next to the bed that he had threatened to kill me with the day before.

I put the scissors next to his jugular vein and raised my hand up ready to strike the final blow on him. A chill came over me and I froze with the words of God going through my mind: 'Thou shall not kill.' Standing looking down at this sewer rat was sickening. I had no thoughts for him now. I just stood there spitting on him till there was no spit left.

Return to Braendam

Erica took me back to Braendam. A few weeks later Islip was arrested for attempting to murder a fellow from our town. I went back to my house with Jackson and tried to get my head level. Islip was looking at a long sentence for this crime – he wasn't getting out of it. I tried to get my life back to some sort of calm. It was very difficult. Islip sent letters saying he was so sorry for everything he had done to me. He only wanted someone to write to him.

Islip got sent to Peterhead prison for seven years. He was sick as a dog and he begged me to forgive him. I went along with anything he said. He couldn't hurt me or Jackson any more. I wrote to him for about a year, then gave up. Why should I write to this monster? He couldn't get to me now but still he sent messages threatening to murder me when he got out.

Death

Time passed. Life was so much better now. I met a fellow but it didn't last long. He was knocked down and killed by a drunk driver. This wasn't happening to me; how would I get through it? I had just started to get over prison and the beatings from Islip and now I was trying to understand death.

What I'm about to write is very painful, so I'm going to be very brief. John died in 1979. I flipped and set fire to the house to get rid of our memories. I got all the neighbours out; they got the fire brigade. I had put Jackson with my neighbour Joanne. I didn't set the house on fire to hurt anyone. Thank God, no one did get hurt. I had got drunk and depressed and had smashed a lamp that was full of flammable liquid into the coal fire. When the lamp exploded it blew out all over the room and set the furniture alight. I had slashed my wrists again and was taken to the police station where they charged me for fire raising and for trying to commit suicide.

The police took Jackson to a children's home. I was taken to a cell that had a camera in it and was told to take all of my clothes off. In front of this camera a policewoman gave me a dirty old blanket to put round my naked body. I would have to stay naked like this till the next morning. I wouldn't get my clothes back till I was up in court. Crying in front of this copper, I said to her, 'Is this what you do to people when they can't understand death?' I was dying inside with the pain of John's death and the loss of my wee lassie. Now the utter shame of this. I couldn't believe John was dead and I was still alive. I couldn't take it in. I sat in that cell with the blanket over my head. I wouldn't come out of the blanket – except once to ask for a fag. They said no. It was cruel. I knew the cops were watching me on camera. Oh God, help me. I'm alive and trying to die. Please help me.

I was taken to court and sent to prison on remand for seven days. This time it was Cornton Vale prison in Stirling; Gateside had been turned into a men's prison. Cornton Vale was a new prison built for the women. I cried for Jackson and John a lot but the shock of setting fire to the house was a nightmare.

When I went back to court the judge let me out on bail. My first stop was to get Jackson, only to be told I wouldn't get Jackson back till after the final court hearing. The court hearing wasn't for months. This did me in – losing John, now my Jackson.

Mental Hospital

I hit the drink and drugs, then slashed my wrists again. I was taken to Dykebar mental hospital on a few occasions and put in a locked ward. I woke up one morning in the locked ward and thought, 'God help me.'

I couldn't stay in here. There was a cage covering the telly so that it didn't get smashed. These poor souls didn't know what day of the week it was. I asked the nurse to phone my mum. She didn't live far away, so she was right beside me in no time, my young sister with her. I said, 'Mum, I'm sorry about all of this. Please tell the doctor if they don't let me out of this ward, I will jump out through the glass window.' Mum knew I would do it. The doctor said he would send me over to the open ward.

This open ward had people like me in there. Slashed wrists, slashed necks, booze and drug problems. I was in Dykebar for a few months this time. I was still waiting to go to court.

When I was released from the mental hospital I started to file for a divorce from Islip. I was twenty-two years old now. I felt as if my heart had been kicked around the world. I was going down south to make a new life. Before leaving Scotland I went to my mum's for a cup of tea. She agreed that it would be better. I told her I would come back for the court case. She looked at me: 'Eve, they won't put you in prison for that. Surely they will understand?' I told her nobody understood me.

Hastings

I went to Hastings with a friend and we found a room. She only lasted a few days, then went back to Scotland. I stayed and got a job in the Queen's Hotel overlooking the sea. It was great. I loved it. The people were nice, the job was nice.

It was a bit better for me to leave Scotland. I wrote letters to Jackson every week. I was really missing her a lot and would have gone to see her. But I was told by a social worker called Miss Black from Paisley social services that I was not allowed to visit my daughter or see her till after the court case. Why was it I got these social workers who had no bloody feelings?

The court case came up. I phoned my mum every week and she told me there was a letter for me to go to court. I froze. I just couldn't go back to jail – no, no, I can't face it yet.

I didn't go to court and had to give up my job and leave Hastings. I wasn't ready to face jail at this time in my life. The shock of the past was just thawing out a wee bit.

It was off to London – another journey. I had a friend there called

Roger. Roger helped a lot, providing the flat for me to live in and looking after me. This I won't forget. I kept a low profile and stayed clear of the police. I went to Alcoholics Anonymous meetings. I had started to go to these meetings in Hastings. The person who told me about A.A. was a man called Tony – an older, wiser person. I liked Tony. He became a good friend. He helped me out a lot in Hastings. When I moved to London I would drop by and see Tony sometimes – not too often in case the police caught me. Tony told me to go back to Scotland and face the charges. He said he would write me a letter to give to the judge. I finally got caught. Tony kept his word and wrote to the judge. I never saw him again. I went back to Hastings to see him but he had gone. I would like to thank him personally. I'll never forget him or Roger, who also helped me a lot.

Cornton Vale Prison

I was sent to Cornton Vale jail for one year for trying to die. Tony's letter helped. If he hadn't written that letter, I think I would have got two years. Back to jail. I was sick. It was like I had been killed and was standing back watching myself die.

Cornton Vale jail, 1979. I walked into the reception. The screw sitting at the desk looked up at me. It was the screw I had spat on in Gateside. I went through the procedure. An officer came in and said, 'I'll take you over to the prison block.' The screw I spat on handed me my tobacco as I was leaving. She was showing me with her actions that she had put the spitting incident behind her. I did the same thing. I thanked her for the tobacco, stared into her eyes, then walked away.

This jail was a lot different. It was brand new. Everything was so modern compared to the old howling Gateside. There were quite a few screws here from Gateside who knew me. But the cells still had chamber pots.

All the cells were in units with a kitchen/sitting room. It looked more like an open prison. The windows in this nick were large squares with fancy bars. This was much better – at least we could see outside clearly. The fencing that surrounded the buildings was high but we could see through that too. The prison is surrounded by lovely countryside.

I was sent to work in the sewing room with my old pal Mrs Heel. I told the screws I didn't want this. They knew about me not liking the sewing room. Why were they sending me back there? Sewing had caused me a lot of trouble. Mrs Heel welcomed me with a dirty, horrible smirk on her face. That was snide. A few days in here, then I will put myself on report. She'll not smirk at me. I put myself on report and told the Assistant Governor I wouldn't go back to the sewing; I would starve to death first.

I was put in my cell. They would come each day and ask me if I was ready to go back to the sewing room. I just looked at them and said, 'I'll starve before I go back there.'

Three days went by. An officer came to take me to see the principal officer, the head of the screws. Miss Reid said to me, 'You can work part-time in the gardens and part-time in the sewing room. Well, this was better than nothing. I said, 'Right, I'll go for that.' I don't know what happened but Mrs Heel didn't like this. She complained. But I never did have to go back to the sewing room. I was allowed to work in the garden party all the time. The garden party had one male screw. There was a civilian officer, Miss Janet Campbell and this little lady was really nice to me. She taught me a lot about gardening and the earth. The wee poem at the start of the book is dedicated to her. I am indebted to her. Working in the gardens was the only thing that kept me sane. If there had been no garden party, I and a lot of other people would have gone mad. We worked in the field, weeding, planting; we cut the grass and grew vegetables. All sorts – lettuce, cucumber, lovely big juicy tomatoes -

– got grown in the big greenhouse. It was good to help grow this healthy food for the inmates.

The time passed very quickly working out here in the fresh country air. One day I saw Miss Campbell working a rotary cultivator. She is only four feet tall, if that. It looked like it was going to run away with her. I walked up to her and said, 'Would you like me to do that?' She was a bit shocked that I offered. Anyway, she showed me how to use the machine. My whole body shook when I used this rotary cultivator. I would pretend it was a therapy to get rid of my disordered confusion

When I was on remand waiting to be sentenced for the fire-raising charge, I saw a head shrink and he told me I had a disordered personality. This didn't surprise me. I could have told him about my disordered personality. I write all through this book about the conflict and confusion. I had inherited this personality from Gateside prison when I was fifteen years old. Those people were all bloody twisted. I thought a lot, working in the gardens, about the past. Some days I would go away down to the bottom of the greenhouse and sit there crying. I cried for Jackson and John.

I wrote to the social worker in charge of Jackson's case. I asked her to bring Jackson to see me. She said she would, but on the condition that I fostered Jackson out. This was the filthiest trick the social work department had pulled yet. I was convinced the Paisley social work department had it in for me. They were saying I wasn't fit to look after Jackson. They thought my crimes were so bad. This new social worker, Miss Black, tells me I can't get Jackson back till she is eighteen years old. Another social work joke.

All this bullshit was doing my head in. The screws were really helpful – they told me to go along with the social worker. They said, 'Do what she says for now.' I did.

I wrote to Black and asked her to bring Jackson on a visit. She brought my wee girl. The door opened and in came Jackson. She ran straight to me, saying, 'Mummy, Mummy.' I was choking back the tears, the pain. This was really my little girl in my arms. It had been a year or more since I had seen her.

She was so lovely looking. The officer started to talk to the social worker. I asked Jackson all about the home she was in. She told me she wanted me to take her home. I whispered into her ear, 'I'll be out of here soon, Jackson. I promise I'll come and get you. You are my little girl, not some stranger's little girl, and I love you.'

It was time for Jackson to go. I had to say this to her: 'Jackson, you will be fostered out. Soon you will be getting a new mummy.' This is what the social worker, Black, had told me to tell my wee lassie. It's sick, isn't it? Poor Jackson looked up at me. I winked at her, then picked her up, saying into her wee ear, 'Don't worry, Jack, I'll get ye back.'

I also got Black to come on a visit to talk about my chances of getting Jackson back. When I asked her if she would help me to get a place to live in for getting out of prison, she told me she couldn't help me. I was a bit shocked. This is part of her job – to help put families back together again. I looked her right in the eye. I saw her for what she really was: another sewer rat who read from books and not from people.

My words to her were, 'Well, Miss Black, I am really sorry you can't help me.' She said, 'Jackson will be in care till she is eighteen years old.' I said, 'You think so?' She said, 'Yes.' 'Okay, then I will have to call up a children's hearing when I leave here. I *will* get my wee lassie back.' Black was taken aback. She left without another word.

I had to go to a children's hearing about fostering Jackson out. What a nightmare! The foster mum was there. My insides were crying out to God. I told the panel it was okay for them to foster Jackson out. This was a terrible thing I had to do. I had to show these people I was thinking of my daughter's future while I was in jail. I *was* thinking of

Jack's future, but not like this. Why be so cruel to me?

That week my young sister Lorraine came to see me. She would visit as much as she could. I was very glad of her visits. She made me laugh. I needed to laugh through all this confusion. Mum paid my sister's train fare to come and visit me as she wasn't very well or she would have come herself. I told Lorraine everything that Black had said and done to me. Lorraine was horrified that Black and the authorities could do this to us.

My mum wrote to me saying, 'Don't worry, Eve. I'll get in touch with the social services and see what the bloody hell they think they are playing at.' My mum had tried to get Jackson into her custody but Black wouldn't let her have Jackson. My mum lived in a tenement building four floors up. It only had one bedroom and five people were living there: my mum, my stepdad, my young sister Natalie, Lorraine and her little boy Derick.

There was no chance of Jackson being put into an overcrowded tenement. My brother Tylar tried to get Jackson. It was useless. He had five kids of his own and he couldn't get her.

Meantime back to working in the gardens, my only sanctuary. Working in the big field eased a lot of the stress, tension and pain. I would walk around crying on my own. The tears wouldn't stop. I would tell my mate, big Maggie, all about the bloody social worker. Maggie was doing life. She was a great lassie to talk to – she always made me feel better. She would crack jokes to make me laugh. That would cheer me up. Here she was, doing life, and she was helping me to keep it together. I cheered up fast and started to make her laugh. I'll never forget Maggie. She was a great mate to know. The time went by quickly, working out here in the fresh air. Lorraine and my mum wrote to me, so did my cousin Kirsty and Carolyn, the lassie that came to court when I was convicted. Carolyn had been a good friend to me when I lived in Barrhead. She never failed to write me a letter every week. Thanks to all the people who wrote. It all helped.

It was time for me to get out of Cornton Vale. I told the Governor I was going to London, not back to Barrhead. Some of the people there would never let me forget my past. A lot of people had hurt me in Barrhead. I couldn't live in that place. I also had hurt people. It would have been a big mistake to go back. I forgive the people who hurt me. I hope they can forgive me for the hurt I caused them. The Governor, who again happened to be Martha Bruce, agreed with me that I should go to London but she was very concerned about me. She told me if I ever needed help to get in touch with her. She had helped so much in the past. When she offered, I thought to myself, 'I am going to make it this time. I'll do it myself.' I was glad of Martha's offer but felt she had done enough for me in the past. How could I ever repay her?

The morning had come for my release. The door opened and in came Janet Campbell – she had come to say goodbye. 'Eve, if you ever need any help when you get out, please get in touch with me.' I gave Miss Campbell a hug and thanked her from the bottom of my heart. I held the tears back when Janet left. That was so nice of her to offer her help. God, I can't be mad if people like Martha Bruce and Janet offer me help. Alexandra worked here in Cornton Vale and I had joined her class as soon as I could. She made me feel safe and came to see me in hospital and also told me that if I needed any help I should write to her. It was overwhelming, all these people who offered help. I had also joined the pottery class this time. I made a lovely mermaid head and gave it to Alexandra. She's still got it to this day. This next poem was inspired by a letter from Alexandra.

Clay

I sat down in the pottery class,
picked up the clay and I was away,
I made a mermaid head.
That to me was life and not death,
out of such darkness a head of light,
out of such madness a delight.

E. McD. inspired by A. Kirkpatrick

I am free, standing in Stirling railway station with an officer, Mrs Athey. She was making sure I got on the train to London. The train pulled up. I thanked the officer and stepped onto the train, waving to her. I felt sorry for her – she was going back to prison.

I am free . . . I am free . . . God, this is a good feeling. The journey to London was wonderful, soaking up this freedom, looking at the hills and braes of Scotland. The train would pass over the border in an hour. I would say goodbye to Scotland for now. Freedom is a gift. I treasure my freedom very much.

I got to London and had to report to a social worker in Arlington Road, Camden Town. I was living in Kentish Town. The social worker, a Miss Dahali Berlin, was the nicest social worker I had ever met. I told her my story of how I lost Jackson. She said, 'Right, we'll get her back.' Dahali liked me – I could tell by her eyes. Was I glad!

I wrote to the children's hearing in Scotland. I asked for a panel to be called up. This would take time. I went to see Dahali every week and made trips to Scotland to see my little girl in the home. Miss Black had tried to foster Jackson but it didn't work out. Jackson had seen me in jail. As far as Jackson was concerned, if she stayed in the home I would come and get her. Jackson had told the social worker, 'If I leave this children's home, my mummy won't know where to find me.' I cried when I heard that.

The time came for the children's hearing. I stayed with my mum and told her I wanted to go to the hearing on my own. So off I went to the children's hearing. Miss Black was there. I spoke to her politely, then we went into the panel. We all talked a lot. My social worker from London, Dahali, had written a good report for me. She wrote that I had a stable, clean flat to take Jackson back to and that I was getting over the death of John. Black was against this. The couple who ran the children's home stood up. They spoke for Jackson and me. Mr and Mrs McMaster thought Jack should be with her mum. This was a dream – these people were helping me. The chairman gave Jackson back to me. I could take her to London.

Black was fuming. She flew off somewhere. I phoned my mum and told her the good news. She was shouting down the phone, 'That's the greatest news, Eve.' I told her about the McMasters helping me; we agreed they were a godsend. I was very indebted to those people.

I told my ma and sister to wait in the train station for my train to come in. The train pulled up in Paisley Gilmour St. There was Mum, my sister Lorraine, her little boy Derick; they all got on the train and we headed for Glasgow Central. We got to Glasgow quickly as it was only a few miles. Now it was on to London for us. I started to laugh, so did my mum. We looked at each other and we all laughed. I had got Jackson back.

My mum said, 'That's it, Eve. I'm going to complain about the way Miss Black has treated you.' Mum phoned the social work department. She was told that Miss Black had gone to live in Canada and would not be coming back. That's Miss Black's answer to me. She ran like a devil was after her. She knew that she was in the wrong.

When my mum told me this, I thought, 'God will deal with her,' then put the woman right out of my head. Jackson and I got on the bus for London. My mum, Lorraine and wee Derick all waved goodbye with big tears in their eyes. It was a sad-happy moment.

Dedicated to Jackson
I lost you once Jack
but I got you back.
I love you always Jack,
and now we'll never part.
Love, Mum.

I wrote these words when I was on the bus back to London with my wee lassie. I had done a very positive thing. It made me feel very good inside. I hadn't felt this good in all my life so far.

Living in London

I got Jackson into school. We kept in touch with the McMasters from the children's home who had helped me. I wanted to let them know how Jackson was doing. I kept in touch with Martha too. She replied to my letters every time. My life began to feel really nice. It was like I had been dead and now I was alive again.

Coming alive again was a good thing. I still had the disordered one but life went okay for me. I still couldn't communicate with people very well. I still got flashbacks of being in jail. I would write and tell Martha about these flashbacks. I had been in London for about one year when I met Katie who became a very good mate. Katie is Irish. She reminded me of one of my mates from the Borstal. Katie helped me a lot. She helped me talk about being incarcerated at such a young age.

It was good to talk with Katie. She made me feel part of the human race again. Thanks, Katie. She is a really special person. I'll always be grateful for all the things she did for me and my family. I met another girl called Liz who had been a battered wife. We would sit in the back garden and share our pain about how it felt being battered wives. I got on very well with Liz. She was a great comfort to me, just as Irish Katie was. I still keep in touch with both of them. We were sitting one Christmas when I had very few Christmas gifts to give to my children and Liz turned up at my front door with her boyfriend Colin. They had two big black bin liners full of Christmas presents for us all. I thought that was one of the nicest things anyone had ever done for me. Thanks, Liz and Colin. There was the girl who lived upstairs from me, Linda; she has a little girl, Jane. Jackson and Jane were the same age and they played together. They went to the same school. Linda was really nice to us, so was her brother Harry. We had tea with them often. I still see Linda and Harry to this day.

Jackson had made friends at school; she started to speak with an English accent; she was happy. This made me happy. I struggled with the flashbacks of prison: the banging doors, the jingling keys, that cold wind that blew around Gateside – still blew around in my head. I had terrible nightmares about jail, and Islip battering me and raping me. It seemed that I would be haunted by jail and this man for the rest of my life. Not forgetting that horrible smear test – another form of rape, 'jail rape'.

I got these words in the middle of the night when I was in Cornton Vale.

God is my heart

God is my heart,
my soul and mind.
I can't see him,
but I feel he is near.
Oh, hear me Lord
as I plead with my heart.
Help me and guide me to my part.

E.McD.

I wanted to write a book about my life and tried to but it got really painful. I couldn't find anyone who would help me in any way. It felt like my brain was strangling. I couldn't trust many people. The injustice of being put in jail was always lingering around in my head. If I could write my story, it would help other people to write theirs. Meantime I hit the drink and drugs. This was bingeing. It would happen every few months when my disordered one would flare up. But it didn't last long.

My big brother David lived not far from London, out in Watford. He would pop over and see me often. David had become a Christian. I was very glad for him; it suited him. He helped a lot of people to find God and a better life. David was always trying to convert me. I went to church with him out in Watford a few times but he never converted me. One time when I went out to Watford to church, after the service David invited me to lunch at one of his friends'. Off we went to have lunch. After lunch I sat in the back garden with Dave's friend Sandy. She took my hand and started to pray to God for me with her eyes closed. I was looking at her. She looked like an angel. I closed my eyes and felt like a great light was upon us. I screamed into my head, 'I am not worthy yet, Lord, to take your hand.' Sandy asked me how I felt. She didn't know what I had said to God. 'I'm all right,' I said.

Then my brother Dave came over to me. He said, 'Eve, what did you see?' I said, 'Nothing.' He wasn't convinced. All that day big D would ask me over and over what had I seen. I finally told Dave what had happened. I told him it felt as if a hand had been offered to me. He said I should become a Christian. I didn't agree with him. I wasn't worthy. Dave said, 'You are worthy.' I told him that my way with God was a bit different from his way. Dave only laughed. I was really glad of David in those days. I didn't feel so alone knowing that part of my family was close by. If it wasn't for Dave I think I would have cracked up and done myself in.

Into the Light

It's now September 1995. A knock on the door startled me – it was a loud knock, a knock of dread. My boyfriend Gary opened the door to a friend. Nelly came into the front room and said, 'Eve, I had a phone call from your dad. He said can you phone him – it's urgent.' I've known Nelly, her husband Johnny and their children for about ten years. Nelly said, 'I hope it's not bad news.' I silently thought that it was bad news. Nelly and Johnny had given my dad their phone number. I didn't have a phone. Johnny told my dad he could ring at any time and Johnny or Nelly would get a message to me. I am very grateful to Nelly and Johnny for letting us use their phone number. They have been good friends to me over the years I've known them.

I went up to the phone with Gary and rang my mum. She told me that my brother David was dead. This was a shock – it wasn't real, I couldn't take it in. I said, 'Mum, I'll ring you back.' I rang my dad. He was in shock. Big D was gone, no . . . no . . .

I went home and stared into the wall. I started to go back in time thinking of how Dave used to protect me when I was little. The tears rolled out of my eyes like a running tap. I turned on the Native American Indian music. I use this music for meditation. I lay on my floor and asked God to help me and guide me to my part.

How are my mum and dad feeling? They have lost a son. Dave loved the ground that my mum walked on. He phoned her every week. I rang my mum again. She sounded really dead inside. She said that my two sisters Lorraine and Rita were coming down to sort out the funeral with me and investigate my brother's death.

We were told that Dave had died of a brain tumour. He was only forty-three years old. He really loved preaching in London's West End. Dave was six feet four inches tall and his voice boomed out. I met people that Dave had brought to Jesus and other people whom he had helped. I was proud of David being a Christian. I told people my brother was a preacher and it's true – he was.

The family all came to my house, including my dad. They came the day before the funeral. Mum could not be there as she is housebound. This was so sad for her; it made my heart twist in pain. The funeral was so sacred to me. I saw Dave three days after he died in the Hemel Hempstead hospital. He looked full of light to me! I hugged him. It was like he was asleep. Then it hit me: he was with God. I said to my two sisters, 'Let's pray for Dave.' I started to pray out for the Lord to take Dave and keep him safe. My sisters looked at me as if I was mad. We all started to leave. I hugged Dave again and said to him, 'That hug is from our mother. We'll never leave you, Dave. You will always be in our hearts.'

I saw Dave again when the family came. We went to see him the night before the funeral. This time it was like Dave's spirit was leaving his body. I didn't say anything to my family; they would have thought I was going mad. That night I saw Dave in a vision. He was my angel. Dave was helping me cope with his death. I stopped crying and felt a kind of peace come over me – sad but nice.

The feeling of peace stayed with me through the funeral. The sun was shining – it had turned out to be a lovely sunny day. David's friends were all there. It was a big turnout. The three pastors of the church preached in turn and some of Dave's friends got up and spoke of him. All through the service I had a feeling that Dave was smiling and walking away with Jesus.

A year before David passed away I had had a really strong vision. I was listening to some of Enigma's music. It was night-time and I was staring at the sky. I went up to bed and lay down. As my head hit the pillow it felt like the top of my head opened up. I put my hands up and felt my head. It was not open, it was only a feeling. It felt like I was being filled up with milk from toe to head. I felt a hand stroke my cheek. My eyes were open. I didn't see a hand, I only had the feeling of it. I got up the next day and felt that I had been filled with the spirit of purity. This was the nicest feeling that I possessed. I told some people about this vision. The look in their eyes told me that they thought I needed help. I told my brother's pastor about it. I know he saw it was the truth. I don't go to church. I don't preach the gospel to people. I found my understanding of God and the Bible through going into my self. That alone is a true mark of the holy spirit. I was dead, now I am alive. I was a sinner with many sins; my sins are forgiven. I know this for sure. My heart has a kind of peace in it now. I never, ever felt that before. I wrote this book with the help of God.

I have been healing myself since I came out of prison in 1980. My method goes like this. First I started to read the Bible. Then I put lovely soft music on and lay down on the floor. I closed my eyes and thought of nothing. It was weird at first. I couldn't just think of nothing as other things were in my head. These thoughts wouldn't go. I kept meditating and started to go back in my life trying to figure out where it all went wrong. I wrote down all my thoughts on my young life. All the wrong things, then all the things that were right. I worked for months on the rights and wrongs of my life. This brought me many tears, a lot of pain. I had to face all my wrongs, all the people that had been hurt by me. I had to forgive all the people who had hurt me. I feel that I am forgiven from the higher power of myself. I hope the people I hurt forgive me. I spent a long time on forgiveness of my soul, of my consciousness. I have rolled round the floor crying and curled up in pain – mental pain.

I worked on myself night and day, trying to understand why I had been torn down. My wrists are all scarred from wrist to elbow. I have a slashed neck. Some of my teeth are missing from the days when Islip battered me. I took the false plate out of my mouth. I stared at it and cried. Every part of my body shook. I was never going to forget what Islip had done to me. My boyfriend Gary saw the pain of this false plate very clearly. We went to my dentist, Mr Sachdev, and arranged for me to have bridges. Mr Sachdev and his associate Laura did the work on my mouth between them. This was one of the greatest feelings: no more false plate. I took a tin of biscuits to Laura and Mr Sachdev to thank them.

Every time I wash my face and see the scars on my arms it's a nightmare. It's worse in the summer. I can't wear short sleeves outside the house. People stare in horror and get scared of me. They move away. My arms can't be fixed like my teeth were. I started to go right into myself with a heavy bag of pain. It felt like all my life's stresses were piled up waiting to get out to be free. This is exactly what happened. One by one I analysed all my wrongs. I looked at myself in the mirror. Was it all my fault? I must work on making things right. I listened to music of every type and danced the pain out of myself. I walked Hampstead Heath for hours on my own. My food intake was little – just enough to keep me alive. Gary helped me through those days. I was so weak I couldn't get out of my bed.

Gary and my children all stuck right by me. I have four children – two girls and two boys – and I consider myself very lucky. Jackson doesn't live at home now. She has her own life but she still keeps in touch. She is twenty-one now and we are good friends. I am so grateful to my family for helping me through those long months of hell.

I feel like a new person and I'm very glad to be writing all of this pain out. I hope that it now ends for ever. I have never done anything worthwhile in my life. I have always felt like I am of no use as many people had said this to me when I was growing up. Islip also made me feel like I was no good.

During this up-rising I am helping people in small ways. My aim is to help people in a lot of ways. My friends Owen and Joanna let me counsel them. We all get help from each other just by talking. The way I see it is that we are all born innocent, so therefore we are all Christians.

I saw a Native American Indian on a T.V. show one night. He said, 'Walk with beauty inside and you will walk with beauty outside.' This man's name is Billy Yellow. He is eighty-seven years old, he runs eight miles a day and he lives near the Grand Canyon in Monument Valley. I would like to meet him one day. I followed Billy's words since the day I heard him say them.

Part of my rising up was helped along by listening to the flute music of R. Carlos Nakai. This recording is called *Emergence*. If you ever come across it, I promise you some special moments will arise from hearing this peaceful music. The music brought out some special drawings from my soul and also some really nice words; these words are poems now. I want to play the flute like R. Carlos Nakai. I wrote Mr Nakai a letter telling him how his music touched me. He didn't answer. I sent Michael Jackson a copy of my poem 'Headflows'. He didn't answer.

'I was once one of the dark, the dying. No one could feel my pain or see me crying.' My brother Tylar wrote those words. I feel and see that I'm out of the dark and into the light. The last lesson that I worked on was to love all people, even the ones I didn't like. I worked on that for some time. If you can love all, then you will know what it's like to feel beautiful inside. To me it felt like the light inside me had been switched on. Thank you great God for helping me, guiding me to my path.

Care

Sometimes we have to believe
in a little magic,
especially
when there is so much pain.

When I think of people
who have nothing,
and I have something,
then I go on.

Faith is never where you think
you'll find it,
but when you do,
it's like flying,
better than giving up and dying.
We are all special in some way
even if it's only for a day.

E.McD.

The bridge to heaven

The bridge to heaven is in us all.
It has to be brought out gently and small.

Bible meetings, peace and love –
an invitation from above.
When you shake God's hand
it will fit like a glove.
The bridge to heaven has a small gate,
The one to hell's great and it could be too late.

This poem came to me as I was reading a letter from my friend Martha Bruce. I dedicate the poem to Martha and thank her for her inspiring letters over the years.

I blamed the Secretary of State for incarcerating me in a prison at such a young age. Now I blame human beings for making these rules without thought. *Words without thoughts never to heaven go.* (Shakespeare). I say it's not about who's to blame. The scars on my arms and my neck have faded a bit, not much. When people see them they ask me how long it's been since I've had a hit. This makes me feel sad. I then have to tell them that I slashed my own arms, that I'm not a heroin addict. Other people look at me with mixed feelings. They back off sometimes. I used to say I was in a car accident, depending on my state of mind at the time. Now I don't have to lie any more.

To all who read and all who need

I the dark warrior who rides from the sun
I the dark warrior who does on earth what should be done,
I ride alone, I ride with known,
I ride through these kingdoms until I am done.

Now dark warrior's time did come,
believe you me this was no fun.
Razor blades in my pocket, now I am on the run.

I the dark warrior fight fire with none,
for I need not slay slayers for their time will come.
I the dark warrior ride as one.

R.McKay and E.McD

After my brother died in September 1995 the time went slowly. It was a great struggle to get anything done in my life. I was in shock still. Christmas Day passed quietly, then came Boxing Day and Gary took the children out for a while. I tried to do some writing. They had only been gone about five minutes when I heard a cracking noise coming from the kitchen. As I walked into the kitchen and looked at the radiator it exploded all over me. With boiling hot, steamy water pumping out all through the ground floor of my maisonette, I automatically ran for the front door and got out. I knocked on my next door neighbours' door, Malika and George, and they rang the fire brigade. Malika's son Whiz went into my house. He tried to shut the kitchen door to stop the water coming into the hall and front room. It was no good. The water was too hot and the pressure of it was too much. I told Whiz to come out.

Gary's voice hit me from the car park. He was shouting and running towards the crowd at my front door. He was shouting, 'Eve . . . Eve . . .' I ran out of the crowd towards him. He was saying, 'Thank God you're alive.' He had seen the steam coming from the kitchen window when he was walking to the house from the car park. Gary thought I was dead, so did my children. They were all crying. It was a nightmare.

The Kentish Town fire brigade turned up. They tried everything to turn the radiator off but the pressure was overriding it all. The radiators were banging and shaking as if a poltergeist was going through them. I was walking in and out of my house not believing what I was seeing. I felt sick and thought, 'What if Gary hadn't taken the children out when he did? They could have been seriously injured or killed.' The firemen finally got the water to stop after about half an hour. Our Christmas and New Year were ruined by this disruption. The family downstairs from me in the basement maisonette got flooded out too. They were opening their Christmas presents at the time. They had gone away Christmas Eve and had just got back when they saw the water come down their walls. The family were put into a bed and breakfast. I was told that as long as my beds were dry I had to stay. I was in shock by now. I didn't give a damn where I was but I still felt the injustice of this.

I felt sorry for the family downstairs. They had come back to a Christmas nightmare. I went down to talk with the family and told them I was really sorry about this. I didn't know what to say; I was still shocked.

Gary and I tried to clean up the mess but it was just too much, so we left the house till the new year. Black stuff had been pumping out of the radiator – it was everywhere. All over the Christmas food in the fridge, in the cupboards; it even stripped the wallpaper from the kitchen and the hall. Some of our neighbours offered to help. Danny gave us a big bag of rags to clean up with. Sue, Barbara and Ruth all offered their help.

I had lived in these flats for eight years and the heating system had never been checked. The communal boiler had broken down three or four times a year. When it broke down we would have to do without hot water and heating for two to three days at a time. The council held a meeting for all tenants on the 8th of January to explain about the heating. A bloke from Seaflame explained that my house was a weak point and that's why my radiator exploded. They had problems with the communal boiler at the time and they had to let it blow.

Camden Council told me I would get no compensation as it wasn't their fault. I went to a lawyer about it over two years ago. The lawyers are still trying. I have no hope. After the explosion we all felt very unsafe in a house that was a weak point. Camden Council would not move us out. It took them till the 10th of January 1996 to get an engineer to come and check all the radiators in the house. Meantime my children had to stay with a friend as we were to scared to stay in our house. Camden Council then took two months to put the radiator back in the kitchen. A new radiator was installed in the front room. I had to save up and do the floor repairs myself. I was sitting here eight months later still waiting on these repairs to be done. I had made appointments with the council for them. I was let down about ten times.

November 1996, the floor repairs have just been finished. Gary has just put the last bit of wood down. We had to buy the wood and do it ourselves. That same month the radiator in the hall starts to hiss. Water starts leaking out of the pipe. We get the emergency people out.

They were here within forty minutes and shut the radiator down. The engineer couldn't believe it; he had come to the last explosion. He said it was bloody ridiculous. All the radiators should have been checked. I told him that the radiators *had* been checked. He just looked at me in horror. I felt like I was back in jail again: no one would help us.

It's January 1997 now. The radiator in the hall is still not fixed. It lies there shut down. I made appointments with Camden Council to have it fixed but again the contractors let me down on three appointments. I don't bother any more. I'm just waiting for the next radiator to blow up. I stressed very strongly to the two area managers that my children and I did not feel safe in this house any more. They took no notice of me or my children. When we hear a noise coming from the radiators, we jump. It's very stressful living like this. I only want to live in safety.

I feel like I'm back in jail living under such stress. When the children ask me why the council won't move us, I tell them the truth: the council don't think the house is unsafe. The children don't understand this. I told them I don't understand it. Communication between tenant and council is not good. I think the council are not too happy with me. I sent a letter to the *Camden Journal* about the flood on Boxing Day 1995. The *Journal* headed the letter 'Why no compassion?'. The council were not happy with this letter. You can see by the way they have treated me since Boxing Day 1995.

Everything that had just happened to us gave me more strength to finish my book. Then I took ill and went to see my G.P., Fred Kavalier. He sent me for tests and I was told I have two fibroid tumours. This was freaky as the doctors don't know the cause of these tumours. I told Dr Kavalier about my book and he said, 'Let me take a look at it and I'll give you my honest opinion.' So I did. A few months later he had read some of it as he is very busy. Fred was very truthful. 'A bit disordered,' he said. I laughed at this. 'You need an educated friend who will help you make some changes and edit the book.' I told him that I had asked people to help, but they couldn't. 'Well,' he said, 'keep going because it's a very gripping and very interesting story.' I went home and attacked my disordered head once again. I am grateful to my doctor for helping. Some months ago met Inna Margiani who lives downstairs. She is educated in reading and writing. After Inna read my story I asked her to help and she was able to help up to page forty-two. We fixed a lot of the disorder, changing some words and improving phrasing. Fate sent Inna to help. What a great friend for me to have. She has taught me a lot about using words in different ways and has a great understanding of my painful life. Thanks for all the help and deep compassion you showed me. Inna saw me very clearly, and this helped me more than words can say.

I wrote this next poem after being inspired by a group called Alpha from Fife, Scotland.

The promise of God
The door to the inner self has only got one handle.
The handle is in the inside of the door.
If you don't turn it – you hide,
If you do turn it – you bide
with the promise of God on your side.

Writing this book alone caused me some very hard thinking and a lot of inner pain. I would like to thank Gary, and Susan and Peter Cornish for making this book possible. These three people donated the computer. I would like to thank the people who wrote me inspiring letters and gave me encouraging words. Martha Bruce's example, for me, speaks for itself.

Sorrow has not been given us for sorrow's sake,
but always as a lesson from which we are to learn
somewhat, which once learned, it ceases to be sorrow.

Carlyle

Eve's story

I was on the earth alone,
I walked for miles and miles.
A lone tree appeared.
I ran to it with open arms,
I hugged it like a child would
hug its mother.

Looking up at the branches,
there shone a lovely apple.
I stared at it, and said, 'No way,
I want to stay. I've seen and been
to hell so tempt me not.
I have not forgotten the forbidden rot,
that an apple could beget.
The love from the tree
is enough for me.
I can go for miles now.
Although the land is dark,
the journey has no end
as I twist and bend.
The flame burns bright,
and guides me into the light.

E. McD. *inspired by*
Mr Corsie and Martha Bruce

To all who read and all who need.

Eve McDougall

Epilogue
Lady Martha Bruce

You have now read Eve's life. What are the issues raised in her story? How did the system fail her and how did she survive?

This is an anecdotal account written in an endeavour to throw more light on to the subject of custody – during and after.

During my sixteen years in the Prison Service, I spoke with many individuals and groups outside prison, and hundreds of women and girls and their relatives inside, as well as countless media persons. To this day I am still astounded by the vagaries of human nature and the ebb and flow of feelings aroused around the subject of women's offences and women in custody.

Coincidentally at the exact time I started to write this chapter the Scottish Office published *Women Offenders – A Safer Way*, a document which should be widely circulated as it at last points up good practice and the fact that women are different, and it starts to tackle the anomalies in the system as they affect women. However, its secondary title 'A Review of Community Disposals', highlights one of my issues.

The custodial setting – the stigma of a custodial setting, being put away, disposed of. I will always remember a parent's answer to a Borstal enquiry form which included the words 'to assist the Court with her disposal'. The mother replied to the effect that she knew her daughter had done wrong and should receive punishment, but surely not be thrown in the rubbish bin. I believe it is no matter what the custodial setting – remand home, youth treatment centre, Borstal, young offenders' institution or prison – the stigma is there, affecting individuals and their families and lasting long after the end of the actual sentence. Only a very small percentage of offenders have committed dastardly crimes. This is especially true of women. Should we not as a society play a more active role in the resettlement after punishment?

Another issue is *the big I AM syndrome* – the cock of the roost, the young person who has done it all and is now exerting pressure on others. There is a flash point when two or more of these individuals land up in the same institution, each with their own following. Eve found herself in this situation during her time in Borstal. Face-saving routes have to be planned, rage ventilated before it boils over into chaos. Inmate culture will never be eradicated and the 'them and us' situation is always present. It is a big factor and greatly affects the positive progress of planned programmes.

Institutionalisation can occur in weeks; those who have experienced stays in hospital know how odd the outside world looks. Imagine the effect of years out of circulation. A woman doing a long sentence once said to me she could happily stay in prison for ever if only she could just get out to the pictures once a week. Prison can form a common bond which is often used for ill but can be turned to good. There is a great need for visitors to prison, people to come in from outside. The Chaplaincy can provide a focus of normality and many enjoyable and helpful schemes take place in the name of the Church.

I don't believe Eve was ever institutionalised but she was certainly very insecure and vulnerable when she left Gateside.

Rules and regulations and lack of facilities are so starkly brought out in Eve's story. Happily, now, under new Acts of parliament, juveniles are no longer sent to prison. The facilities at Cornton Vale Women's Prison are vastly superior to those then available at Greenock. Rules and regulations are essential for security and the management of institutions but it is when lack of facilities and shortage of staffing exist that rules become a mockery and frustration can set in for all concerned.

Eve is very direct in writing of her encounters with staff. Prison staff are the backbone of management: it is their interaction with each other and the inmates that can reduce tension and create an atmosphere of co-operation so necessary if anything at all is to be achieved. All must be led to understand each other's business and work as a team. Relationships formed are the start of a trust which may lead on to the maturing of personalities. The staff at Greenock and Cornton Vale really got to know the women and girls but had to be ever mindful of the setting in which they worked. I once asked a life sentence prisoner what had been important to her. Her answer: 'The milk of human kindness.' Kindness is not leniency, for leniency can prove disastrous in a prison.

I found it was on night visits and at weekends, when there was more time to speak individually with staff, that I could regain focus on the needs yet to be met.

So we come to after-care and *social work intervention*. Eve was in Greenock during the period of changeover from prison welfare to social work units being established in all prisons. A residential training order carried no statutory after-care provision. A great many girls regarded their probation officer as the person who put them inside and then recalled them to serve their full time. The new system did much to assist the development of through-care and for the first time provided a co-ordinated approach between agencies. Later in her story Eve experiences the benefit of social work intervention.

The Governor of a prison is walking a tight-rope, ever mindful of security, government policy, public opinion, victims, media attention and the known needs of the inmate population. Risks have to be taken if the meeting of inmate needs is to lead to proper rehabilitation. Custody should not be isolated. There is a before, during and after. Thought needs to be given to the dilemma of balance between retribution and rehabilitation. There is often betrayal on both sides. It is good that the authorities have at last grasped the fact that, in Scotland, the small number of women who require custody make it a manageable problem – although only manageable if the need for active co-operation from all agencies is understood and made possible. The management of an institution must always be based on the needs of the individuals contained within it.

Perhaps I may digress a moment to explain a little about population and needs.

In my time of working in the Prison Service, the greatest number of women in custody were there either on remand or doing very short sentences. Many were recidivists and their offences related to abuse of alcohol. For some we could do no more than set them back on their feet and encourage them to attend AA meetings, but, if time allowed, we ran a six-week alcohol dependency course which made them look at their problem and introduced them to caring agencies outside.

The Borstal and Young Offenders' programme was run in modules and developed considerably over the years. It was important to show these girls that they could be trusted and with the co-operation of the Girl Guide movement a Ranger Guide unit was introduced whereby girls could do community service and work alongside other young people.

Long-term prisoners need stimulus and support in facing guilt and understanding the true meaning of forgiveness both in relation to themselves and those they have hurt. The Chaplaincy is important. Our Deaconess ran Sunday evening meetings, with visiting speakers, which were recognised by the Church of Scotland Woman's Guild.

In the introduction I wrote of recording progress in the last twenty years – in terms both of progress by Eve herself and the developments in which I took part.

Firstly, had Eve gained anything to outweigh the tremendous damage done to her mentally by her stay in prison? We were almost totally unprepared for the influx of juveniles from the courts. Whilst we could ensure that they were unlikely to escape, we had to devise methods, within very limited resources, to try and provide the training to which they were entitled. Part-time education, mothercraft, talks with a psychologist, a daily job were all we had to offer. One girl went out daily to school and others did community work with handicapped children, but this all depended on their previous history of absconding and their own wishes. If Eve had been able to join in one of the wonderful camps run for us by the Iona Community at Camas, Isle of Mull, she may have discovered more of her talents. Others took part in the expeditions with the Six Circle Groups organised and developed by Charles Hills. Borstal boys and, later, young offenders and prisoners undertook community projects together with less able youngsters from Rudolf Steiner schools and youngsters on probation.

It is these groups and many others and even individuals that provided a network of continuing voluntary care known to us and available for use by such as Eve. She kept in touch with me by correspondence, told me of her marriage and in distress sought help when she was pregnant and being beaten. All this is explained in her story.

In 1969 it had been announced that a new women's prison was to be built. Working parties were set up, decisions made and finally a site agreed. Cornton Vale at Bridge of Allan, near Stirling, was built by a contractor using Borstal boys trained in their own institutions by prison officers. Materials were constructed in yet other prisons. It was a period of fruitful activity and I consider myself extremely lucky to have been part of it. Much was achieved by a great number of people during the building, planning and development of Cornton Vale. It gave room to move, enormous possibilities for growth and a sure and certain challenge.

As Eve recalls she returned there on remand and for a short prison sentence. I remember how disturbed she was, her joy at a reunion with her daughter and our discussions of the future. Despite her unhappiness she had matured and it is interesting in reading her account to see how much better she could deal with her period of detention and her decision to go to England.

Again she kept in touch by letter over the years, telling me of additions to her family, her health and activities, till finally she arrived with her family to see me. They are a great family – a credit to her. It was during that visit that plans were laid to write a book. She visited the next year with the manuscript and the venture commenced.

Time marches on, the type of prisoner changes and revised regimes become essential. Some of the basic problems are now better understood.

Has the way of dealing with women offenders in Scotland become safer? Are we moving into the light? Only the next decade will tell.

Afterword
John Harvey

For two years during my time as Parish Minister in Stirling, in the late 1970s, I served as Prison Chaplain in Cornton Vale Women's Prison. Martha Bruce was Governor, Norma Ronald was Deaconess – two remarkable and influential women. I probably met Eve then, although I cannot remember her.

Both before and after that period, and indeed up to the present day, my wife and I have had a personal involvement with Braendam Family House near Thornhill, which played a not insignificant part in Eve's story. Another remarkable woman – Lilias Graham – was the inspiration for that house, now part of the international ATD Fourth World movement.

And for the whole of my ministry (nearly thirty-five years now) I have been a member of the Iona Community, serving at different times both as Warden of the Abbey on Iona and as Leader of the Community; so I am also aware of the work referred to by Martha Bruce in relation to the Community's camps at Camas on the Isle of Mull.

None of the above, of course, makes me professionally qualified to comment on Eve's story; but it does give me a very strong personal interest, as you can imagine. Her story – tragically, in many respects such a common story for far too many young women in Scotland today, and yet at the same time unique in its insights and articulation – both angered and inspired me. It reminded me of a saying I came across recently, by the second-century Christian theologian St Augustine of Hippo: 'Hope has two beautiful daughters, Anger and Courage; Anger at the ways things are, and Courage to see they do not remain the way they are.' I read it in a week when five suicides were reported in Scotland's prisons; an appalling statistic, of which we should be thoroughly ashamed as a society. But hope is what we need, if this is going to stop; and hope, as defined by St Augustine, is what we get, I think, as we read what Eve has to tell us.

I want to draw out five main themes from what Eve has written. (The fact that they all begin with 'P' tells you more about me as a preacher than anything else!)

First, *punishment*. When we think of prison, and prisoners, in a general sort of way, we think, I suppose, of punishment. But the truth is, of course, that our society punishes the Eves among us long before they get to prison. We punish them by our willingness to allow the continuance, as if there was no alternative, of the social conditions and the educational conditions in which Eve and others are brought up. We persuade ourselves that there is no alternative; we piously mutter Jesus' words about 'the poor being always with you' for excuse, taking them entirely out of context; we use the (true up to a point) fact that many people survive such conditions and never fall foul of the law as an argument for doing nothing to deal with the conditions which do contribute to the troubles of the likes of Eve; and we still seem, as a society, to act on John Major's notorious dictum after the Bulger case, when he said that we should 'condemn a little more, understand a little less'.

This, it seems to me, is something more than just the result of a culture of denial. It certainly is that: the denial of responsibility, as a society, for those on the margins, either through pretending that they don't exist, or through blaming them for the conditions in which they do exist. But I think it's more positive than that. There seems to be, within our culture or within our human nature, or perhaps a mixture of both, a twisted desire to kick those who are down. One of the lessons that my time at Cornton Vale taught me, very quickly, was the true nature of punishment. I came to see that, for most of the inmates, punishment had started long before they came through the gates of the prison. It had begun, most often, in their childhood. It had continued, for so many of them, through all sorts of abusive and failed relationships with parents, teachers, social workers, partners, employers, police – and it had only culminated in the particular offence which brought them, through our judicial system, into jail. To recognise this is in no way to deny the serious nature of their offences, nor is it to fail to acknowledge the pain and injuries – sometimes fatal – that they had wrought on their victims, or on society. But for most of them that too, in their heads and in their hearts, was part of the punishment. How do you live with the knowledge that you have smothered your aged mother because you could no longer cope with her, or plunged a knife into the stomach of your partner in a drunken brawl? And how can you understand what is happening to you when, at fourteen, after a rather messy childhood, you find yourself in jail – on remand – because society really hasn't bothered to think out what else to do with you?

Which brings me to my second 'P' – *place*. For most of the inmates I met in Cornton Vale, the immediate punishment was of course their loss of freedom – whatever that had meant to them – once the gates shut behind them in the jail. I don't suppose anyone can really understand what that means, unless you have experienced it. Never to go anywhere alone; never to be able to make choices; keys and locks all the time;

routine, routine, routine; and, as Eve's story shows only too well, masses of seemingly petty and meaningless rules. Plus the exposure to total strangers, and the uncertainty always present about how they are going to react to you, or you to them. And the fear.

But what Eve's story also shows, of course – and this has been increasingly impressing itself on the consciousness of society in recent months, as a result of the spate of prison suicides in Scotland – is something that the Prison Service and all who work in it have known, and flagged up, for years. And that is that prison is often the wrong place for some offenders against the law.

It is the right place for many, of course. And as I have already indicated, the work of the prison staff with many inmates, for whom it is the right place, has often produced life-changing results. I saw that in Cornton Vale. I have also seen it in the Barlinnie Special Unit. But that unit, and its undoubted success in so many cases, precisely makes my point. Our prisons, as they are presently constituted, are mainly designed to contain. The fact that, despite that, the staff do so much good rehabilitation work, doesn't help. Contain – and, in many cases, continue the punishment – that's what the majority of our prisons are designed for.

But what we need, as a society, is something else besides. Yes, we need places where violent and destructive people can be contained – securely, so as not to be a danger to society, or to themselves. What we also need are places where people who are not needing that sort of long-term containment, or who are not fundamentally violent and destructive, can find the security and continuity within which, in the company of professional workers, they can address the real issues of the world in which they have to live, and learn how to cope with them. Of course that happens, quite often, in our prisons as they are. But not always; and, in recent months in Scotland, we have seen in these suicides the tragic results of it not happening.

What then are we talking about? Mention has already begun to be made of bail hostels or units, where people – often young ones who should not be in prison – can be placed for as long as it takes. Clearly this issue needs much more airing by those who have far more knowledge of the system than I. But clearly also it will need public airing. Because if we are to deal with this problem of place – and who would doubt, reading Eve's story, that it desperately needs dealing with – then we have to raise public awareness of the problem, so that the political will can be found to do something about it.

So to the third 'P' – *politics*. What we do about our prison system, and indeed about our whole system of criminal justice, is a highly political issue. The balance, at the moment, and for as long as I can remember, has been on the side of containment and punishment. So the political approach has been to have more prisons built along these lines; we have had an emphasis on tough regimes; short sharp shocks; and the main concern of the politicians seems to have been to 'save the taxpayers' money'.

This political approach is both ineffective and shortsighted. It doesn't actually deal with the problem of people offending. Certainly it locks them away for a while, and during that time staff do what they can. But read Eve's story. Sense the frustration in the conversations she records with some of the staff who sought to help her. Think of what could have been done if more money had been available to provide both Eve and the staff with better facilities for tackling her problems. And consider the question: Which is the better value for money? A system that focuses primarily on containment or punishment, or a system that focuses primarily on prevention and rehabilitation? The experience of the Barlinnie Special Unit has shown that careful thought and intelligent planning, combined with appropriate financial and personnel resources, set in the context of the best in professional practice, can produce life-changing results even with people regarded as the most violent and intractable members of society. Why wait until people get to that stage before spending our resources on them? Prevention, we all know, is better than cure.

But nothing will change unless the politicians are willing to change it. Prison staff can do so much. Charitable and statutory bodies can do so much. Individuals can do so much. Until we collectively make it clear that we want a change in the way our society's resources are spent, so that the matter is dealt with in a fundamental way, all the above people and bodies will have to continue to run in order to stand still, with perhaps just a little bit of progress every so often.

Will the coming of the Scottish Parliament help? Criminal justice, the prosecution system, police and prisons will all fall within its remit. As we move towards this, various bodies are encouraging the people of Scotland to say loud and clear what values we hold dear as citizens in Scotland today, and what values we want the new parliament to embody. Perhaps this is one of those defining moments in a society when we actually have a chance to change things for the better at a very basic level, rather than accept a tinkering with things, a shuffling of the pieces on the board. For the sake of the Eves of our coming Scottish society, and indeed for the sake of all of us, we had better take that chance. Politically.

My fourth 'P' – *partnership* – arises both out of my reading of Eve's story and out of my experience of the international ATD Fourth World movement, to which Braendam House at Thornhill belongs.

A brief word, firstly, about the movement. ATD – *Aide à toute detresse* – was started by a French priest, Fr Joseph Wresinski, after the Second World War. Sent to work in the refugee camps around Paris, and himself a child of a very poor family, Wresinski came to commit his life to working alongside the very poorest families of the world. He called them the inhabitants of the *Fourth World*, taking the title from the language of the French Revolutionary period, when the people of the *Quatrième Monde* were the ones whom nobody consulted, the ones at the bottom of the pile; if you like, *Les Misérables*.

Since its inception, ATD Fourth World has grown to a worldwide movement, with the status of a UN Non-Governmental Organisation, and has been successful, for instance, in having October 17 named by the UN as the annual Day for the Eradication of Poverty. More significantly, it works at two levels in many countries, including Britain. On the one hand, it seeks to influence government policy in relation to poverty issues, which in fact it sees and promotes as human rights issues, by trying to bring together politicians and planners with the real experts in poverty, those who live in it. On the other hand, its volunteers work alongside people who live in poverty, as partners, sharing the goals of support, of understanding, of articulation and of transformation.

Now I doubt if anyone can read Eve's story without being struck by two things in particular about her: her intelligence and her articulation skills. Yet time and again, as her story shows, she has been treated as someone who lacked both. Time and again, Eve speaks of the way her experiences in and out of prison affected her mind. 'My imagination was so alive'; 'Mentally I could go anywhere'; 'I felt inside out'; 'I was getting scared of my thoughts, I wanted to die'; 'Borstal was all head games'; 'My thinking was beginning to swing'; 'I still had the feeling of doom in my gut'; in these and in other phrases of the book, we cannot escape the fact that we are dealing here with an intelligent young woman who is struggling to understand what is happening to her, and finds it both hard and terrifying.

My point here is not that it is surprising that Eve was and is an intelligent person. Nor am I making a comment on the way her mind was being affected. Rather I am pointing to the fact that she was so often treated as if she was *un*intelligent, as if, having been sent to jail, she was *de facto* stupid, thick, slow, unable to learn. Labelled a failure, she was treated as one – and so came to believe, for a long time, that that was what she was.

Out of its long experience of working in partnership with people in poverty, one of the things the ATD Fourth World movement has come to value is the insight that nobody needs to carry the label 'failure'. Indeed, time and again the people who come to be part of ATD from the world of poverty tell how, in partnership, 'the labels come off'. Yet Eve's whole experience was of labels. She was labelled a criminal, useless, a failure, before she was hardly an adolescent, never mind an adult. She was thrown into a world of labels – social worker, screw, inmate – and had to fight all the way to see through the labels to the people behind them. And it was only as individual people began to treat her as a person in her own right, and not simply as a label, a number, a statistic, that life began to change for Eve, for the better. Partnership made a difference.

But why should we be surprised at this? After all, that is our normal daily experience as human beings. And so I come to my fifth, and final, 'P' – *people*. Shining through Eve's story come the names of the people who made the difference to her life. Not all of them affected her in a positive way, for example Miss Cool, the social worker – 'Cool + McDougall = loss of freedom' is how Eve describes the relationship at one point. But many did. Aunt Greta. Mrs Heel, 'a very cold woman but I must admit she was a good teacher'. Miss Alexandra Kirkpatrick – 'a great teacher and a really nice, understanding woman'. Lynn, Carrol, Mag and the other girls who helped her to get through Borstal. Mr McConnell who 'would tell us mad jokes to keep our morale up'. Erica the psychologist. Tylar, Eve's brother; and of course the Guv'nor, Martha Bruce, and Lilias Graham at Braendam. And Jackson. And John.

'Being with people,' says Eve at one point, 'helped me a lot. Even if they didn't talk to me a smile was a good treat for my soul.' Towards the end of the book, I began to wonder if Eve was going to 'get religion'. The thought, I'll readily admit, did not appeal. But thankfully it gradually became clear that what Eve was getting was not 'religion', but insight. This was of course being mediated through people. And the insight that was growing in her was growing in the best way – from the inside out.

In her poems, Eve tries to express this. Thus, in one, she writes:

The bridge to heaven is in us all
It has to be brought out gently and small.

In another, she explores the same theme a bit more fully, with:

The door to the inner self has only got one handle.
The handle is in the inside of the door.
If you don't turn it – you hide,
if you do turn it – you bide
with the promise of God on your side.

And in a third, entitled Care, she writes:

Faith is never where you think
you'll find it
but when you do
it's like flying.
Better than giving up and dying.

I'm not sure Eve would thank me if I were to say that in these and other pieces in the book she is actually expressing what 'spirituality' is about. It has been said that 'spirituality is what ultimately motivates you'. That can only come from the inside – not from any merely outward observance, or from obedience to a God or a religion entirely 'out there'. It has to be grown within, from below. In the end, as Eve herself says, what ultimately motivated her was that much-abused word, love. 'The last lesson that I worked on' – after all the horror of the labelling and abuse and the imprisonment and the sense of failure and the many wrong choices she made, and the loss and the bereavement and the pain – 'the last lesson that I worked on was to love all people, even the ones I didn't like.' She goes on: 'I worked on that for some time.' It will probably be for a lifetime, Eve!

In her book *The Children We Deserve* Rosalind Miles writes: 'If children don't get what they deserve, they become adults whom no society deserves, and who no individual deserves to be.' One of the lessons that the Iona Community has taught me – perhaps the one I am most grateful for, the one I most need to keep on being reminded of – is the connectedness of life. It has taught me the connectedness of the sacred and the secular – that there is no division between prayer and politics, between work and worship, and that this world and the next are closely intertwined. More recently, that lesson has begun to sink in more deeply to my understanding of human life – all human life, including my own. I begin to see more clearly, even if I don't fully apprehend the consequences of it, the connectedness between my child and my adult, my inner and my outer self.

Eve, it seems to me, knows more about this than I ever did at her age, probably more than I do even now. That said, however, if this story is to be read as more than just the story of one young woman's journey through hell towards life, then we need to read in it about the connectedness of many things. Certainly, it is about the connectedness between crime and punishment, and between punishment and rehabilitation. It seems to me it is also about the connectedness between a society's values and the way it apportions its financial and other resources. It is about the connectedness between the majority in a society, who feel relatively secure, and the minority, who feel relatively vulnerable. It is about the connectedness between individuals – either through labelling or through loving. It is about the connectedness between the child and the adult in us all. In the end of the day, it is also about the connectedness between us as human beings and that which ultimately motivates us; which some of us, with Eve, call God.

Some words used in this book:

aye	yes
cannae	cannot
chippie	chip shop
copper	police officer
Feagie	Feruslie Park
fleeing	drunk
gaff	a place
greetin	crying
Guv	Governor
heid	head
hoose	house
lifted	arrested
lum	chimney
Maw	Mum
meat wagon	police van
message	errand
naw	no
oor	our
peter	prison cell or police cell
piece	bread and butter
piss pot	chamber pot
polis	police
polis motor	police car
scheme	housing complex
screw	prison officer
wee lassie	small girl
wee laddie	small boy
ya	you

Also from Wild Goose Publications . . .

COLOURS OF HOPE AND PROMISE
Personal stories of HIV and AIDS
Brid Cullen

The simple yet often moving accounts in Brid Cullen's book come from ordinary people who have been affected by HIV and AIDS in different ways. The courage and determination of all these individuals shine through as an encouragement to those who have just been diagnosed and their friends and families, showing that HIV and AIDS need not mean dying but rather living to the full.

128pp. ● 1-901557-09-X ● £8.99

STARTING WHERE WE ARE
The story of a neighbourhood centre
Kathy Galloway (ed.)

BOOK AND AUDIO CASSETTE PACK

The story of the Orbiston Neighbourhood Centre is one of innovation, energy and success as a community project.

The approach taken was based on the principles of Liberation Theology – a methodology of change and empowerment which originated in Latin America and for the first time has been explored in a thorough way in Scotland.

104 pp ● 1-901557-04-9 ● £12.00 ● book and cassette pack

To receive our full catalogue, please contact:

Wild Goose Publications
Unit 15, Six Harmony Row
Glasgow G51 3BA

Tel. 0141 440 0985 Fax 0141 440 2338

The Iona Community

The Iona Community is an ecumenical Christian community, founded in 1938 by the late Lord MacLeod of Fuinary (the Revd George MacLeod DD) and committed to seeking new ways of living the Gospel in today's world. Gathered around the rebuilding of the ancient monastic buildings of Iona Abbey, but with its original inspiration in the poorest areas of Glasgow during the Depression, the Community has sought ever since the 'rebuilding of the common life', bringing together work and worship, prayer and politics, the sacred and the secular in ways that reflect its strongly incarnational theology.

The Community today is a movement of over 200 Members, around 1,500 Associate Members and about 700 Friends. The Members — women and men from many backgrounds and denominations, most in Britain, but some overseas — are committed to a rule of daily prayer and Bible reading, sharing and accounting for their use of time and money, regular meeting and action for justice and peace.

The Iona Community maintains three centres on Iona and Mull: Iona Abbey and the MacLeod Centre on Iona, and Camas Adventure Camp on the Ross of Mull. Its base is in Community House, Glasgow, where it also supports work with young people, the Wild Goose Resource and Worship Groups, a bimonthly magazine (*Coracle*) and a publishing house (Wild Goose Publications).

For further information on the Iona Community please contact:

The Iona Community
Pearce Institute,
840 Govan Road
Glasgow G51 3UU
T. 0141 445 4561; **F.** 0141 445 4295
e-mail: ionacomm@gla.iona.org.uk